INSTITUTIONAL TRAUMA

This book develops a critical psychological account of trauma as an institutional phenomenon, which is currently missing in psychological discourse.

While a great deal of attention has been paid to understanding trauma in individualized terms, comparatively little attention has been paid to understanding trauma as a feature of institutions. Based on the observation that experiences of trauma are deeply lodged in institutional conditions, this book asks what comes into view when psychological trauma is approached as an institutional phenomenon. Recognizing that the personal is political, this book proposes an expanded institutional analytic of trauma and lays critical foundations for responses that treat institutions as sites of trauma and its management. Drawing on a range of disciplines including critical psychology, feminist theory, postcolonial studies, and critical trauma studies, this expanded institutional analytic advocates for institutional transformation within and beyond the confines of dominant psychological knowledge(s) and practice.

Institutional Trauma is fascinating reading for academics, students, practitioners, and anybody interested in understanding institutional power, violence, and harm.

Lucy Thompson is a critical feminist psychologist who studies institutional power relations and their impacts from the perspective that the personal is political. From this perspective, she specializes in feminist analyses of institutions, violence, and psychological distress. Her research has made methodological, empirical, and conceptual contributions in these areas. Specifically, she has published an analytical framework, Feminist Relational Discourse Analysis, which allows critical examinations of the personal-political dimensions of experience. She has also studied institutional phenomena such as imposter syndrome and workplace violence from this perspective. Her conceptual work in the domain of institutional trauma reflects her commitment to understanding experiences of psychological distress as institutionally bound.

Concepts for Critical Psychology: Disciplinary Boundaries Re-thought

Series editor: Ian Parker

Developments inside psychology that question the history of the discipline and the way it functions in society have led many psychologists to look outside the discipline for new ideas. This series draws on cutting edge critiques from just outside psychology in order to complement and question critical arguments emerging inside. The authors provide new perspectives on subjectivity from disciplinary debates and cultural phenomena adjacent to traditional studies of the individual.

The books in the series are useful for advanced level undergraduate and postgraduate students, researchers and lecturers in psychology and other related disciplines such as cultural studies, geography, literary theory, philosophy, psychotherapy, social work and sociology.

Most recently published titles:

Chatbot Therapy
A Critical Analysis of AI Mental Health Treatment
Eoin Fullam

Developing Recovery Pathways for Mental Health Disorders through Creative Coproduction
A Case Study of Anorexia Nervosa
Jean Haslam and Mita Sykes

Institutional Trauma
A Critical Psychological Perspective on Power, Violence, and Harm
Lucy Thompson

For more information about this series, please visit: www.routledge.com/Concepts-for-Critical-Psychology/book-series/CONCEPTSCRIT

INSTITUTIONAL TRAUMA

A Critical Psychological Perspective on Power, Violence, and Harm

Lucy Thompson

LONDON AND NEW YORK

Designed cover image: Getty © Yuriy Bucharskiy

First published 2026
by Routledge
4 Park Square, Milton Park, Abingdon, Oxon OX14 4RN

and by Routledge
605 Third Avenue, New York, NY 10158

Routledge is an imprint of the Taylor & Francis Group, an informa business

© 2026 Lucy Thompson

The right of Lucy Thompson to be identified as author of this work has been asserted in accordance with sections 77 and 78 of the Copyright, Designs and Patents Act 1988.

All rights reserved. No part of this book may be reprinted or reproduced or utilised in any form or by any electronic, mechanical, or other means, now known or hereafter invented, including photocopying and recording, or in any information storage or retrieval system, without permission in writing from the publishers.

Trademark notice: Product or corporate names may be trademarks or registered trademarks, and are used only for identification and explanation without intent to infringe.

British Library Cataloguing-in-Publication Data
A catalogue record for this book is available from the British Library

ISBN: 9780367487256 (hbk)
ISBN: 9780367487249 (pbk)
ISBN: 9781003042471 (ebk)

DOI: 10.4324/9781003042471

Typeset in Sabon
by codeMantra

Dedicated to Professor Marcia Worrell

CONTENTS

Series preface		*ix*
Acknowledgments		*xi*
1	Introducing Trauma	1
2	Genealogies of Trauma	15
3	Trauma Capitalism	39
4	Institutions	67
5	Institutional Trauma	88
6	(De)Theorizing and (Re)Imagining Institutional Trauma	111
7	Into Trauma's Negative Space	137
Index		*145*

SERIES PREFACE

Psychology as a discipline is, of necessity, embedded in a variety of institutional contexts across the realm of the psy complex, institutional contexts that warrant its power and close down space for thinking otherwise, what Lucy Thompson terms in this searing review and critique of trauma's 'negative space.' This reliance of psychology on institutions in order, despite the best intentions of well-meaning psychologists who would like to think outside the frame of psy complex, to exercise power, violence, and harm, is profoundly paradoxical. For, as this detailed feminist critical psychological examination of the production and reproduction of trauma points out, psychology routinely individualizes trauma, resilience and forms of adaptation, and adaptation of the human subject it models in its studies to traumatizing social conditions.

To accomplish the critical task this book sets itself and accomplishes with such scholarly energy, one must, of course, find a way of tracing and thus disconnecting ourselves from the manifold contradictory forms of ideology that, at one moment, reduce social-political phenomena to the level of the individual and, at the next, prescribe adaptive normative social relations that are of a piece with heteropatriarchal and capitalist images of the world. This book reframes mainstream psychological research on trauma as 'institutional trauma,' in an argument which recenters the role of social relations in the production and reproduction of trauma and also recenters the role of critical psychological resistance to these images of the human being that are at stake.

This book is thus in tune with Theodor Adorno's rather cryptic statement that every human image is ideology, except the negative one. The argument about the crucial role of 'negative space' in challenging institutional trauma breathes new life and meaning into that statement, showing us that the hypocritically 'positive' forms of psychology that repetitively trap us in individualized trauma discourse can only be challenged and undone by insisting on a feminist critique of ideology, of institutions, feminist critical psychological critique that is opened up by thinking otherwise, claiming negative space as our own.

Psychology in general, and the 'psychology of trauma' in particular - case in point in this book - always organizes its conceptualization, research, data, interpretations, and explanations of human behavior; to engage in critique of psychology is, therefore, to understand how that organizational process works. In order to step back from the pernicious assumptions that psychology makes about our lives, assumptions that are then reiterated as 'findings' produced within constrained, carefully organized, conditions, we must, then, be able to analyze and expose that organizational work, understand how the institutions that house psychology home in on the 'individual,' and limit our view of wider cultural-historical conditions.

The feminist critical psychological standpoint of this book is also, of course, intersectional, grasping how the pathologization of individuals who are brought within the frame of 'trauma' are not only, as an institutional condition of orthodox disciplinary psychological research, gendered, sexed, in order to make them visible to psychologists, but also racialized, subject to colonial presuppositions about which kind of human beings count, the ways they count. This book gives us a valuable inside account of the production and reproduction of 'institutional trauma,' inhabiting the frame of psychology, but viewing it from within the 'negative space' it opens up. It thus takes us into the discipline while also taking a distance from it; it is 'outwith' psychology as all good critical psychology should be.

Ian Parker
University of Manchester

ACKNOWLEDGMENTS

To Ian Parker: Thank you for encouraging and welcoming this book. More than this, thank you for your work to sustain the discipline of critical psychology over the decades. To Jeanne Marecek: Thank you for supporting the original grain of this idea and for publishing it in *Feminism and Psychology*. Thank you too for the long coffees about this book across the ether.

To Bridgette Rickett, Katy Day, and Kate Milnes: Your contributions to this book lie in my very being, which will always be soundly and carefully critical. Thank you, Katy, for supporting this work from the start. Thank you, Kate, for your guidance when it became impossible to ignore that *the personal is political*, and for dancing at my wedding. Thank you, Bridgette, for your guidance, intellect, patience, and love, and for standing with me in the hardest times of my life. To Jem Tosh, who I have traveled with personally and professionally for over a decade: Thank you for supporting this book from the very beginning. For your existence, your work, and your friendship, I am eternally grateful. To the Intersectional Violences Research Group, Lois Donnelly, Tanya Frances, Lisa Lazard, and Emma Turley, who were beside me as I wrote this book: Thank you for your unending brilliance and kindness. To Rose Capdevila: Thank you for your enduring encouragement, generosity, and friendship as I have built my life in feminist psychology. To my treasured colleagues Jenna Watling Neal and Kristen Upson: Thank you for your solidarity, and especially for our writing time, which gave me the space and permission to do this work. To two magical thinkers, Lisa Szymecko and Wenda Bauchspies: Thank you for your humanity, brilliance, wisdom, and imagination. To Jonathan Weaver, Katie Clements, and Sarah Prior: Thank you for being a harbor of hope.

Thank you to my dear friends, Jessica Drakett, Jennifer Park Jaquint, Emily O'Brien, Daniel Drakett, Daniel Jaquint, Daniel O'Brien, and

TJB, who cared about this book, asked questions, and lived its process with me in times of joy, adventure, celebration, pain, and sorrow. To Carol Pierce: Thank you for helping us all the time and knowing what really matters in life. To Karen Babayan and Chris Taylor: Thank you for being our family, and for the home you have given me, where I chose to write these acknowledgments. To Christine Atha: Thank you for supporting me in the most wonderful and difficult times, and for showing me what I could accomplish. To Glyn Thompson: Thank you for opening up other worlds, and for making me think.

To Rocky, my closest companion, and Adam, the love of my life: Thank you for your endless and relentless love.

To anyone who has felt the crushing pain of institutions, this book is for you more than anyone.

1
INTRODUCING TRAUMA

This book is about psychological trauma. It is about how trauma is understood and how it can be imagined. The central argument driving this book is that while trauma is heavily tied to institutional conditions, dominant Euro-American research and practice tend to focus on trauma at the level of the individual. This argument rests on the fact that a substantial amount of attention has been paid to understanding trauma on an individual basis, and this informs a range of 'trauma-informed' responses and interventions. In contrast, the same attention has not been paid to the institutional conditions surrounding experiences and understandings of trauma. In this book, I argue that an institutional orientation is needed in order to address these conditions. Specifically, this book is an invitation to imagine the possibilities for understanding and action that come into view when trauma is approached as an institutional phenomenon.

Introducing Trauma

While the definition of 'trauma' may seem obvious or self-evident to some, trauma carries a vast array of meanings. The concept of trauma is so culturally fluid and expansive that 'trauma' is now widely used to describe an array of experiences, from notions of psychic shock to traumatic events, personal catastrophe, collective injury, or tragedy; often in the same breath (Fassin & Rechtman, 2009). This fluidity extends to psychiatric definitions of trauma, which have shifted across various iterations of diagnostic criteria (Leys, 2000; Smith & Freyd, 2014). Practitioners have noted that trauma has become "shorthand for the effect of all types of painful experience" (Afuape, 2011, p. 42). As such, it has been argued that we are living in an 'age of trauma' (Kurtz, 2018). In this era, notions of 'trauma' are used to simultaneously describe events and their impacts, where "the trauma [event] has caused a trauma [reaction]" (Tseris, 2019a,

DOI: 10.4324/9781003042471-1

p. 687). Here, "we find ourselves using the language of trauma easily; and often with a very powerful and felt sense that we know what we mean when we do so" (Stevens, 2011, p. 175). As a result of its ubiquity, trauma has thus become anchored in broad, taken-for-granted meanings and assumptions that inform how it is understood and interpreted:

> trauma has taken on the logics of the icon. When we imagine we are "seeing" trauma or the signs of its passage, we know immediately that something spectacular and catastrophic has transpired and we fear, also with a sense of immediacy, that normal systems for understanding the event and any of its survivors will be overwhelmed and rendered incapable of adequately capturing its immensity or the subtlety of its sublime pervasiveness.
> *(Stevens, 2011, p. 176)*

However, underneath this 'icon' are very specific meanings and assumptions derived from the Euro-American psychological disciplines, or *psy disciplines*. Indeed, it has been observed that the dominant Euro-American trauma concept is a "neo-colonial imposition" that functions to marginalize and silence localized understandings and responses to distress (Segalo, 2015, p. 447). Such dominant meanings and assumptions are rarely questioned in broader popular discourse or by those who take up dominant psychological concepts. This has led to the rise of dominant perspectives on trauma, which prioritize particular ways of understanding trauma and obscure others. Outside of Eurocentric thought, trauma is imagined as a collective, cultural, and political condition (Visser, 2018). However, in Europe and North America, just as the concept of 'mental health' has been claimed as property of the dominant psy disciplines (Khúc, 2024), so too has trauma. Here, dominant interpretations of trauma are informed by psychotherapeutic individualism (Kaye, 1999). There are now countless academic articles, blogs, best-selling books, coaching manuals, toolboxes, social media hashtags, workbooks, and more, which apply this dominant lens to explain what trauma *is* (and, by proxy, what it *is not*). This has generated a wealth of knowledge and resources for those seeking to understand and address trauma, which have been taken up under the mantle of 'trauma-informed' care, education, therapy, and a host of other practice-based applications. Within this knowledge base, biopsychiatric discourses underpin interpretations of trauma as an individual pathology.

Dominant Euro-American Interpretations of Trauma

Dominant interpretations of trauma in Europe and North America are rooted in powerful biomedical assumptions. These interpretations conceptualize trauma as a series of individual 'symptoms.' And, while psychological distress – including trauma – can be understood on a continuum including biological, moral, social, and relational perspectives, individualized interpretations typically dominate public discourse and mainstream psychological theory, research, and practice. Subsequently, a wealth of attention has been paid to understanding and responding to the experience of trauma on an individual and granular level. More specifically, dominant interpretations of trauma prioritize a focus on biology and the brain, concentrating specifically on brain structure and function, memory, and neurobiological development.

The most dominant claims about trauma within Euro-American societies largely draw on biopsychiatric discourse. Biopsychiatry is a specific clinical perspective that adopts a disease model and locates psychological distress as a brain-based pathology, where disease is defined as "impaired functioning as a consequence of physical and chemical changes" (Lewis, 2011, p. 88). There are multiple psychiatric models, but biomedical perspectives tend to dominate psychiatric discourse (Lewis, 2011). And, while psychiatry is distinct from the discipline of psychology, the power of biopsychiatric discourse means that the two are typically conflated in broader cultural spaces through an assumption that psychological phenomena – and particularly psychological distress – are best interpreted in a biopsychiatric way. This mode of psychiatry is enmeshed with biomedicine, to the extent that "the only real difference between biomedicine and biopsychiatry is the specificity of the disease" (Lewis, 2011, p. 88). From this perspective, psychiatric disease is viewed as a disadvantageous, abnormal, pathological deficit (Lewis, 2011). Lewis notes that, as such, this approach situates pathology as a consequence of a 'broken brain' (Andreasen, 1984).

This biopsychiatric perspective informs popular rhetoric that invites professionals to treat psychological distress as a physical ailment. In one common example, appeals are made to professionals and the public to treat 'mental illness' as they would treat a broken leg. Therefore, therapeutic responses to trauma have become arranged primarily around the goal of identifying and treating specific 'symptoms' in isolation from the complex socio-political entanglements of people's lives. Even when these entanglements are recognized, biology and individual-level symptoms are the ultimate site of intervention (Tseris, 2019b). In the case of psychological distress, and trauma more specifically, the dominant biopsychiatric perspective has been criticized for ignoring the role of these entanglements. As Segalo (2015) observes, a focus on individual psychological symptoms is problematic because "it tends to reduce complex problems to psychological terms" and "puts a clinical cast on problems that are political, economic and socio-historical" (Segalo, 2015, p. 447).

Therefore, while the biopsychiatric approach was initially intended to reduce the stigma surrounding psychological distress by attributing it to biological causes beyond an individual's control, it had the unfortunate effect of prioritizing biological explanations at the expense of all else. Rather than viewing diverse psychological and psychiatric perspectives as complementary – and recognizing that no single perspective can ever explain a phenomenon in its entirety – this approach has taken up a dominant position, obscuring a range of complementary perspectives that would allow for more comprehensive and nuanced understandings of psychological distress. Such narrowing is harmful because it locates psychological distress primarily in biology and places distress in a vacuum outside of socio-political relations. This additionally rests on the problematic assumption that physiological disease itself takes place in a vacuum, which contradicts extensive evidence of the social, environmental, and socio-political determinants of health, including poverty (e.g., Bullard, 2000; Hodgetts & Stolte, 2017). The problem that arises here, then, is that biopsychiatric perspectives are both dominant and limited in their ability to explain psychological distress. In this book, I will examine the dominance of biopsychiatric perspectives on trauma and consider ways of imagining trauma beyond these confines. In doing so, I will shift the focus onto socio-political relations by examining how institutions shape understandings and experiences of trauma. This examination begins with the observation that *the personal is political*.

Feminist and Critical Psychological Interpretations: The Personal Is Political

This book arises from concerns over dominant biopsychiatric interpretations of psychological trauma and - in response - draws on a range of interdisciplinary perspectives to imagine trauma beyond these realms. This response is grounded in feminist and critical psychological perspectives, which focus on the socio-political contingency of psychological experiences and knowledge(s). These perspectives draw on the fundamental feminist recognition that "the personal is political" (Hanisch, 1970, p. 76). In this formative work, Hanisch argued that "personal problems are political problems" (Hanisch, 1970, p. 76). More than 40 years later, feminist theorist Sara Ahmed observes along similar lines that:

> The personal is structural. I learned that you can be hit by a structure; you can be bruised by a structure. An individual man who is given permission: that is structure. His violence is justified as natural and inevitable: that is structure. A girl is made responsible: that is

structure. A policeman who turns away because it is a domestic call: that is structure. A judge who talks about what she was wearing: that is structure. A structure is an arrangement, an order, a building; an assembly.

(Ahmed, 2017, p. 30)

Recognizing that *the personal is political*, Ahmed directly names this dynamic in the form of socio-political structures and their personal impacts. Here, she construes individual acts as manifestations and expressions of those structures. Within this dynamic, personal experiences and acts are inextricable from socio-political conditions and the power arrangements they create. Ahmed's examples conjure several institutional scenes wherein trauma looms, with specters of gender-based violence, police violence, and victim blaming within and beyond legal institutions. While these personal-political dynamics are central to the phenomenon of trauma, they are glaringly absent in dominant biopsychiatric interpretations. For this reason, the feminist observation that the *personal is political* underpins the institutional orientation of this book.

Feminist psychological perspectives are valuable in their ability to situate knowledge, experience, and psychological phenomena in relation to socio-political conditions. However, these perspectives have been marginalized in psychological discourse and research. One profound consequence of this has been a proliferation of largely de-politicized accounts of psychological experiences and phenomena. In response, feminist psychologists have worked to elucidate the interplay between these domains. To give an example, I have done this in my own work, developing Feminist Relational Discourse Analysis (FRDA) (Thompson et al., 2018) to situate individual experiences in the discursive realms of which they are made.

Along with this focus on the personal and political dimensions of psychological experiences and phenomena, feminist psychological perspectives also offer and invite a critical reorientation of psychology itself. In tandem with critical psychology, feminist psychological perspectives have deconstructed dominant psychological knowledge to illustrate the specificities of claims that are otherwise presented as self-evident, universal truths. For instance, Crawford and Marecek (1989) argue that science itself is "a social institution subject to normative influences" (p. 479). Identifying these specificities reveals the underpinning assumptions of scientific claims, their scope, and the interests they reflect and serve. In turn, this reveals what they do not or cannot account for, and the implications of this. In line with critical psychological perspectives, this form of analysis shows how language, discourse, and power fundamentally drive everyday meanings and knowledge production, including scientific inquiry. Such analyses are concerned with exploring the constructions and representations of phenomena that give them their meaning and invite particular kinds of response and action (e.g., Hare-Mustin & Marecek, 1990; Parker, 2015; Potter, 1996).

Drawing on an array of "critical tools" (Burman, 1992, p. 46), feminist psychologists subject psychological knowledge to this mode of deconstruction and analysis. Burman (1992) outlines three principles along these lines. The first principle involves identifying the specificities and contingencies of dominant theorizing in psychology; connecting this to socio-historical and socio-political conditions to show how particular ideas reflect dominant power interests. For example, Burman describes how sexology has theorized versions of female sexuality that reflect notions of passive femininity and promote the regulation of female sexuality on this basis (Burman, 1992). As McClelland (2017) observes, "one of the key interventions of feminist psychology has been to interrupt dominant assumptions about how concepts are defined" (p. 451). The goal of such efforts is to show the specificities of totalizing and universalizing theories in order to disrupt their dominance (McClelland, 2017).

The second principle renders the 'truth' claims made by dominant theories problematic on this basis, reframing universalizing claims as socially constituted and provisional:

> Rather than knowledge being seen as universal, eternal and value-free, we can now show it to be provisional, culturally and historically specific, and both arising from and contributing to social interests.
> *(Burman, 1992, p. 46)*

Burman gives the example of psychological distress, arguing that contemporary categories and practices surrounding mental health and the medicalization of distress rest on the historical development of theory about the psychological subject, which culminated in the "birth of the psychological individual... with a corresponding development of male professionals... and the abstracted and androcentric subject of psychological theory" (p. 46). This notion of the self-contained individual, which will be discussed further in Chapter 2, should therefore also be viewed as specific rather than universal; as one rendering of selfhood among many.

Burman's third principle rests on the critical recognition that these constructions of the self-contained individual obstruct political analysis, instead favoring a de-politicized mode of selfhood that can be regulated as such (Burman, 1992). This critical recognition reveals how:

> the rational, unitary subject that typifies western individualism and inhabits our social and psychological theories is a model of modern man… and [how] the assumption of the separate, autonomous subject is structured into our tools of measurement, whether we are measuring patterns of consumption or personality traits.
> *(Burman, 1992, p. 47)*

In response, Burman proposes an epistemic reorientation, viewing knowledge(s) as discursively produced and associated practices as specific forms of regulation. Such regulation manifests through conceptualizations of a psychological subject who then serves as the site of analysis and intervention.

Burman's analysis therefore invites critical interrogation of de-politicized constructions of psychological selfhood and the separation of the personal and political that is accomplished therein. This shows how the separation of the individual from the political domain in the dominant psy disciplines is an active accomplishment rather than a consequence of simple observations of 'reality.' Indeed, even the most cursory everyday observations of this 'reality' indicate quite clearly that the personal and the political are tightly intertwined. On this basis alone, it should be absurd to argue that socio-political conditions have little bearing on psychological experiences, or at least that these conditions are not important enough to warrant serious and sustained attention in the way that the individual does. Nevertheless, mainstream psychological perspectives have systematically prioritized the study of the individual in isolation from these conditions.

A Feminist Psychological Response to Trauma

The prioritization of the individual as both the site of analysis and intervention has been a long-standing problem in responses to psychological distress. Indeed, the separation of the individual from socio-political conditions formed the ground from which Hanisch (1970) spoke against individualized responses to her own psychological distress in her original articulation of the claim that *the personal is political*. Here, she exclaimed, "women are messed over, not messed up! We need to change the objective conditions, not adjust to them" (p. 76). My goal in this book is therefore to imagine responses to trauma beyond dominant perspectives, with a specific focus on socio-political conditions.

Feminist psychological perspectives are well-placed to drive such responses, primarily because they enable imagination beyond dominant individualized and universalizing interpretations of trauma. The point here is not to supersede or eradicate other forms of knowledge, but instead to imagine the possibilities outside of these. Here, I follow in the footsteps of feminist psychologists who have centered marginalized perspectives in response to dominant and universalizing claims:

> I open up ways of thinking and theorizing about bodies, consent, therapy, and medicine, but do not attempt to reduce that complexity or generalise the specific to the majority. Instead, I focus more on those stories least told in discussions of rape and abuse, as well as within medical contexts. This analysis is an opening up of perspectives, not the 'last word' (or worse yet, an authoritative one). Acknowledging that certain perspectives and experiences exist, is not the same as claiming it is the *only* one, or even the most predominant one, but continues the feminist practice of centering the perspectives of the marginalised.
>
> *(Tosh, 2020, p. 17)*

In doing so, I advocate for localized and specific institutional knowledges of trauma generated from such perspectives. Thus, the goal of this book is not to try to define 'Trauma' in one way or another, but rather to interrupt dominant assumptions about trauma and develop institutional approaches instead. Rather than setting out a universalizing framework, this book articulates an institutional orientation that can be applied to generate situated understandings of and responses to trauma in deep recognition of these specificities.

Feminist psychological perspectives are also well-placed to drive such responses because they question the practice of generating universalizing theory. For instance, in 2021, I wrote *toward* a feminist psychological theory of institutional trauma to question the epistemic grip of biopsychiatric and individualized theories of trauma (Thompson, 2021). Here, the practice of writing *toward* theory spoke to the impossibility of arriving at a universal or totalizing theory. Taking heed of critical psychologist Rachel Liebert (2019), who deconstructs and resists the practice of theory generation itself, my goal was not to reach theory, and reflected a deep discomfort with the imposition of theoretical boundaries and enclosures. In her profound work of anti-theory, Liebert critically interrogates the "desire-to-know" (p. 12) that drives the project of scientific theory construction, arguing that this *desire* to know – and to know in a particular way – represents the colonization of experience and phenomena by theory and its specific assumptions. Indeed, "to Know was and is to capture, own, control – whether ideas, plants, peoples, or lands" (Liebert, 2019, p. 78).

In this sense, Liebert argues, the project of scientific theorizing itself becomes imbued with the goals of colonization (Liebert, 2019). Dominant claims to 'Know,' then, reflect, and reveal epistemic power and privilege. Indeed, as Liebert argues: "Coloniality is dependent on a hierarchy of Knowing, Knowers, Knowledge" (2019, p. 78). And, while their claims are partial, dominant theories often make universalizing claims that appear to represent the 'truth' or 'reality' of their objects of study. Thus, my response will be driven by a specific discomfort with bounding knowledge around trauma as mainstream perspectives do. There is a certain hypocrisy in attempting to loosen the grip of one theory by tightening the grip of another. So, while I argue that the concept of 'institutional trauma' is under-theorized, I also recognize that this may be preferable since theorization can enable epistemic dominance, exclusion, and violence. The feminist psychological response of this book therefore recognizes and resists the potentials for epistemic injustice that lie in epistemic dominance.

As Miranda Fricker has observed, epistemic dominance controls the forms of understanding and interpretation that are made available in broader cultural spaces (Fricker, 2007). Hermeneutical injustice arises when those dominant forms of interpretation render others unavailable, constraining how a particular experience can be understood (Fricker, 2007). Mimi Khúc (2024) observes how dominant psychological perspectives coalesce into hermeneutical injustice and invites resistance in response:

> the stories I had been told… were not only wrong but also the very structures that shaped why life felt unlivable for me. And so I turned my eye to those stories and asked where they came from, and how they harm…
>
> I asked, what else is hurting us, invisibly, that we internalize as individual pathology to be individually overcome? I asked, what alternative stories might we tell about ourselves, about our suffering and our healing, and what new languages would we need to do so?
> *(Khúc, 2024, p. 9)*

Overview of This Book

This book aims to develop an institutional interpretation of trauma and invite responses that focus on the personal and political dimensions of trauma that are typically absent within dominant interpretations.

Writing as a critical and feminist psychologist with expertise in institutional theory and a PTSD diagnosis, my aim is to explore what falls back from dominant interpretations; out of focus and unnoticed. I view this as the *negative space* around dominant Euro-American biopsychiatric interpretations of trauma. In this book, I argue that this *negative space* is institutional. That is: institutions are always giving shape and meaning to understandings and experiences of trauma, but at the same time remain out of focus.

This book is therefore a direct invitation to imagine the possibilities and responses that come into view with an institutional analytic. This institutional analytic is offered in contrast with dominant individualized interpretations of trauma, which primarily imagine the individual as the site of trauma and its management, and promote individual intervention and transformation on this basis. Here, I will articulate an institutional analytic as a different orientation to trauma, which views institutions as sites of trauma and its management. In doing so, I will explore the responses that come into view with an institutional analytic, and advocate for institutional intervention and transformation in response.

The institutional analytic I propose in this book rests on the claim that trauma can be defined as institutional in at least two key ways: through its construction and position as an object of institutional knowledge (and knowledge production), and through its experiential (re)production with/in institutional power relations. Here, I will recognize that understandings and experiences of trauma are institutionally specific and bound. I will therefore advocate for imaginings of trauma beyond dominant individualized and universalizing Euro-American perspectives. I ground this argument in the specific observation that dominant notions of trauma are a "neo-colonial imposition" (Segalo, 2015, p. 447), which function to obscure localized understandings and responses to distress. In response, I will draw on a range of perspectives to consider ways of imagining trauma otherwise.

In line with these concerns, the first overarching aim of this book is to critically examine dominant biopsychiatric theories of trauma and where they come from. Taking this position means that I will consider but intentionally avoid directly citing some key texts that have engaged in authoritative practices of epistemic domination – including some very well-known books in this area. This is in line with a broader feminist politics of citation, which recognizes that citations form the basis of knowledge production, and that, therefore, feminist citational practices should reflect a desire to build feminist knowledge (Ahmed, 2017). Where such texts are cited, it is for the purpose of critical analysis rather than endorsement.

The second overarching aim is to broaden notions of 'trauma,' what we can 'know' about it, and how we can 'know' this. To accomplish this aim, I will specifically focus on articulating how understandings and experiences of trauma are lodged in established institutional power. The third and interrelated aim is to resist the dominance of individualized, de-politicized, and pathologizing knowledge about trauma and disrupt taken-for-granted assumptions that represent this knowledge as natural or self-evident. In response, I will pursue the fourth aim, which is to invite situated and specific responses grounded in the understanding that knowledge(s), experiences, and claims are institutionally situated (as opposed to universal), specific (as opposed to generalizable), and in flux (as opposed to stable).

Summary of Chapters

In Chapter 2, I will begin by articulating *institutional trauma* in the first sense, defining trauma as an object and product of institutional knowledge. To articulate trauma in this sense, I trace the development of dominant knowledges about trauma in the Euro-American psy disciplines and their implications for understandings of trauma. The aim of this analysis is to critically examine dominant trauma paradigms and concepts. Here, I will examine the two most dominant interpretative frameworks of trauma to understand "the ways in which some iterations of the trauma concept are involved in covering up complexities, promoting professional agenda, and reducing the range of experiences and responses that are able to be considered" (Tseris, 2019b, p. 7). On these grounds, I will argue that what is *meant* by trauma in any given time and place is partial and specific, reflecting dominant paradigms and their interests. I then turn to critical and feminist psychological perspectives to imagine trauma knowledge(s) as inherently institutional.

In Chapter 3, I will examine the institutional practices that bring dominant knowledge(s) and conceptualizations of trauma to bear and consider their consequences. In doing so, I will argue that dominant conceptualizations of trauma provide *prescriptive logics*, which set out specific instructions for how trauma should be understood and addressed. I will begin by examining the broad institutional practices of psychiatrization (e.g., Mills, 2014; Rose, 2019), pathologization (e.g., Parker et al., 1995), and privatization (Thompson, 2021), and consider how these practices constitute what is referred to as *diagnostic imperialism* (Rose, 2019). I will also examine how this supports what has been referred to previously as the 'trauma industry' (Afuape, 2011), which regulates experiences of – and responses to – trauma. I will then broaden this analysis to argue that the trauma industry can be viewed as an expression of what I will call *trauma capitalism*: a set of socio-political and economic relations that leverage trauma in the interests of capitalism. In the last part of Chapter 3, I will critically consider the consequences and implications of trauma capitalism from feminist and critical psychological perspectives. Specifically, I will focus on how trauma capitalism cultivates cultures of resilience, silence, and recovery.

In Chapter 4, I turn to institutional theory to show how understandings and experiences of trauma are institutionally bound. Here, I will introduce institutions and argue that powerful institutions constitute the fundamental grounds on which trauma can be experienced, understood, and 'treated.' I will also argue that this is not sufficiently accounted for in the mainstream psy disciplines. In response, I will present an expanded definition of institutions and discuss some examples of institutions that are centrally implicated in the (re)production of understandings and experiences of trauma. These will serve as illustrative examples to show how an expanded institutional analytic of trauma can be applied. I will argue on this basis that there is a pressing need to develop institutional approaches and responses to trauma, rather than focusing primarily on the individual as the site of trauma and its management.

Chapter 5 is a consideration of *institutional trauma* in the second sense: through its experiential (re)production with/in institutional power relations. Here, I will critically evaluate prior considerations of institutions as they relate to trauma, based on the expanded analytic of institutions discussed in Chapter 4. I will also consider the extent to which these theories conceptualize institutions as sites for intervention and transformation. Based on this evaluation, I will propose an institutional analytic of trauma to articulate the experiential (re)production of trauma with/in institutional power relations and conceptualize trauma as a relational and situated institutional phenomenon. In doing so, I will outline a need for conceptual tools that enable institutional intervention and transformation. Here, I will again be guided by the need for institutional intervention and transformation in response to trauma, which I proposed in Chapter 4.

In Chapter 6, I will apply the institutional analytic developed in Chapters 4 and 5 to develop an institutional response to trauma. Guided by a recognition of the dominant Euro-American trauma concept as a "neo-colonial imposition" that functions to marginalize and silence localized understandings and responses to distress (Segalo, 2015, p. 447), I will imagine what an institutional analytic of trauma can bring into view, moving beyond dominant assumptions about the boundaries of individuals, trauma, and institutions. The goal in this chapter is not to lay claim to trauma by solidifying a new scientific theory or way of knowing. Rather, this chapter serves as an invitation to explore what I refer to as the *negative space* surrounding trauma, and imagine how we can approach trauma outside of dominant conceptualizations. To do this, I will invoke a range of conceptual tools that can bring the institutional realms of trauma into view and allow for institutional intervention and transformation. As with the examples of institutions discussed in Chapter 4, these are by no means comprehensive. Rather, they provide examples among many others that can be invoked to bring institutions into focus as sites for intervention and transformation.

Chapter 7 serves as an invitation to consider the opportunities that arise in the *negative space* surrounding dominant conceptualizations of trauma. In this chapter, I will engage in hopeful speculation to consider what it means to explore this negative space and imagine trauma otherwise. Specifically, I will consider the opportunities for imagination and hermeneutical justice that lie in this space. As such, this chapter serves not as a review or conclusion, but as a portal into the possibilities of this negative space. Here, I advocate against theoretical formalization and instead consider the possibilities for institutional understanding and transformation that come into view through such explorations. This unraveling and (re)imagining aims to loosen dominant interpretations and refocus attention beyond these. As such, I will argue that *negative space* brings us to 'loose ends', or strands of exploration, that cannot be tied up with certainty and are instead open to interpretation. Therefore, rather than serving as the 'end' of this book, this chapter will form a launching point into the negative space of institutions for future work.

References

Afuape, T. (2011). *Power, Resistance and Liberation in Therapy with Survivors of Trauma: To Have Our Hearts Broken*. Routledge.

Ahmed, S. (2017). *Living a Feminist Life*. Duke University Press.

Andreasen, N. C. (1984). *The Broken Brain: The Biological Revolution in Psychiatry*. Harper & Row Publishers.

Bullard, R. D. (2000). *Dumping in Dixie: Race, Class, and Environmental Quality* (3rd ed.). Routledge.

Burman, E. (1992). Feminism and discourse in developmental psychology: Power, subjectivity and interpretation. *Feminism & Psychology*, 2(1), 45–59.

Crawford, M., & Marecek, J. (1989). Feminist theory, feminist psychology: A bibliography of epistemology, critical analysis, and applications. *Psychology of Women Quarterly*, 13, 477–491.

Fassin, D., & Rechtman, R. (2009). *The Empire of Trauma*. Princeton University Press.

Fricker, M. (2007). *Epistemic Injustice: Power and the Ethics of Knowing*. Oxford University Press.

Hanisch, C. (1970). The Personal is Political. *Notes from the Second Year: Women's Liberation*, 1(1), 76–78.

Hare-Mustin, R. T., & Marecek, J. (1990). *Making a Difference: Psychology and the Construction of Gender*. Yale University Press.

Hodgetts, D., & Stolte, O. (2017). *Urban Poverty and Health Inequalities: A Relational Approach*. Routledge.

Kaye, J. (1999). Toward a Non-Regulative Praxis. In I. Parker (Ed.), *Deconstructing Psychotherapy* (pp. 19–38). Sage Publications Ltd.

Khúc, M. (2024). *Dear Elia: Letters from the Asian American Abyss*. Duke University Press.

Kurtz, J. R. (2018). *Trauma and Literature*. Cambridge University Press.

Lewis, B. (2011). *Narrative Psychiatry: How Stories Can Shape Clinical Practice*. Johns Hopkins University Press.

Leys, R. (2000). *Trauma: A Genealogy*. The University of Chicago Press.

Liebert, R. J. (2019). *Psycurity*. Routledge.

McClelland, S. I. (2017). Conceptual disruption: The self-anchored ladder in critical feminist research. *Psychology of Women Quarterly*, 41(4), 451–464. https://doi.org/10.1177/0361684317725985

Mills, C. (2014). *Decolonizing Global Mental Health: The Psychiatrization of the Majority World*. Routledge.

Parker, I. (2015). *Critical Discursive Psychology* (2nd ed.). Springer.

Parker, I., Georgaca, E., Harper, D., McLaughlin, T., & Stowell-Smith, M. (1995). *Deconstructing Psychopathology*. Sage Publications.

Potter, J. (1996). *Representing Reality: Discourse, Rhetoric and Social Construction*. SAGE Publications Ltd.

Rose, N. (2019). *Our Psychiatric Future*. Polity Press.

Segalo, P. (2015). Trauma and gender. *Social and Personality Psychology Compass*, 9(9), 447–454. https://doi.org/10.1111/spc3.12192

Smith, C. P., & Freyd, J. J. (2014). Institutional betrayal. *American Psychologist*, 69(6), 575–584. https://doi.org/10.1037/a0037564

Stevens, M. E. (2011). Trauma's Essential Bodies. In M. J. Casper & P. Currah (Eds.), *Corpus: An Interdisciplinary Reader on Bodies and Knowledge* (pp. 171–186). Palgrave Macmillan.

Thompson, L. (2021). Toward a feminist psychological theory of "institutional trauma." *Feminism & Psychology*, 31(1), 99–118. https://doi.org/10.1177/0959353520968374

Thompson, L., Rickett, B., & Day, K. (2018). Feminist relational discourse analysis: putting the personal in the political in feminist research. *Qualitative Research in Psychology*, 15(1), 93–115. https://doi.org/10.1080/14780887.2017.1393586

Tosh, J. (2020). *The Body and Consent in Psychology, Psychiatry, and Medicine: A Therapeutic Rape Culture* (1st ed.). Routledge.

Tseris, E. (2019a). Social work and women's mental health: Does trauma theory provide a useful framework? *British Journal of Social Work*, 49(3), 686–703. https://doi.org/10.1093/bjsw/bcy090

Tseris, E. (2019b). *Trauma, Women's Mental Health, and Social Justice: Pitfalls and Possibilities*. Routledge.

Visser, I. (2018). Trauma in Non-Western Contexts. In J. R. Kurtz (Ed.), *Trauma and Literature* (pp. 124–139). Cambridge University Press.

2
GENEALOGIES OF TRAUMA

In Chapter 1, I argued that trauma can be defined as institutional in at least two key ways: through its construction and position as an object of institutional knowledge (and knowledge production), and through its experiential (re)production with/in institutional power relations. In this chapter, and in Chapter 3, I will critically consider trauma as institutional in the first sense; through its construction and position as an object of institutional knowledge (and knowledge production). In this chapter, I will begin by examining the psychological theories and assumptions underpinning dominant biopsychiatric interpretations of trauma. I will then critically examine the two most dominant interpretative frameworks of trauma: *PTSD* and *neurobiology*. I will do this by tracing the institutional production of these frameworks to examine the discursive production of trauma itself. In doing so, I will show how 'Trauma' became an object of institutional knowledge and knowledge production. On these grounds, I will argue that what is *meant* by trauma in any given time and place is not all that is or can be *known*, but rather a specific representation of trauma reflecting (and privileging) particular ways of 'Knowing' (Liebert, 2019). To synthesize this analysis, I turn to critical and feminist psychological perspectives to imagine trauma knowledge(s) as inherently institutional. On this basis, I will then propose an institutional analytic of trauma to articulate trauma as institutional in the first sense.

Mainstream Psychology's Trauma Knowledge(s)

Dominant conceptualizations of trauma in the mainstream European and North American psy disciplines are broadly grounded in the philosophical assumptions of an individualized biomedical model. This biomedical model, originating from Europe and North America, underpins

DOI: 10.4324/9781003042471-2

dominant discourses and perspectives on psychological distress and what has been termed 'pathological' (Canguilhem, 1978; Rose, 1985; Tosh, 2016). This philosophy is so dominant that it is often presented as the 'truth' about trauma. This medical model was formally enshrined as foundational to the psy disciplines in Europe during the 17th to 19th centuries. Known as the 'Age of Reason' and the 'Age of Enlightenment,' this specific period was characterized by an expansion of knowledge production based on the principles and value(s) of empiricism and rationalism. During this period, empiricism and rationalism were imposed as 'superior' ways of knowing, both within and beyond the confines of Europe (Tosh & Carson, 2016). During this time, scientific discourse subjugated established ways of knowing to become *the* authoritative means by which to interpret behavior and define and classify 'normality' and 'abnormality' (Gone, 2008; Tosh, 2016). This included the redefinition of sanity (Spivak, 1988).

Formally institutionalized in a shift from classical to modernist epistemes, this mode of knowing was presented as radical and liberatory, grounded in the application of principles from the natural world to human societies (Spary, 1999). This "naturalizing sleight-of-hand" (Spary, 1999, p. 281) borrowed taxonomic and comparative systems from the natural sciences to establish similar hierarchies in social realms, including the distinction, classification, and ordering of race, gender, class, age, and other socially relevant categories (Spary, 1999; Stevens, 2011). However, while this intellectual 'revolution' was presented as liberatory, it constituted a new form of cultural imperialism:

> Within this culture, both nature and enlightenment were functional terms, rather than descriptive ones. Both were normalizing and universalizing: providing standards for behavior that extended far outside the realm of polite society.
>
> *(Spary, 1999, p. 274)*

One clear marker of this form of imperialism was the imposition of particular standards for behavior. Here, normalizing and universalizing frameworks were anything but: in fact, they were extremely specific and reflected the values and power of whiteness. They were, as Khúc (2024, p. 15) puts it, "white as fuck."

Rose (1985) traces the specific formation of European and North American psychology during this Enlightenment period. In doing so, he identifies and debunks several dominant claims and received wisdoms about the development of psychology as an 'objective' science. For instance, contrary to definitive histories, which locate psychology in ancient philosophical traditions, Rose situates the institutionalization of modern European and North American psychology as a much more recent and distinctive 'event' with a specific purpose:

> there is a common acceptance that something significant occurred in a period from about 1875 to about 1925... in Britain and Western Europe as well as in the United States, which has the character of an 'event'. This event appears to consist of the translation or extension of certain recurrent questions about the nature of humans from the closed space of philosophy to a domain of positive knowledge: the formation of psychology as a coherent and individuated scientific discourse.
>
> *(Rose, 1985, p. 3)*

In contrast with dominant claims about psychology's objective observations and interpretations of individual behavior, Rose (1985) argues that this psychology of the individual was created through a coordinated program of intervention, which actively produced an individualized psychological subject with/in scientific discourse and transformed the complex human experience into an observable, isolated, individuated phenomenon. Rose (1985) also debunks dominant narratives that chart a discipline concerned with "the normal mental functioning of human beings" (Rose, 1985, p. 1), arguing instead that "psychological knowledge of the individual was constituted around the pole of abnormality" (p. 5). On this basis, Rose (1985) contests a central claim of psychology: That knowledge about the abnormal and pathological has been generated through an accumulation of knowledge about the 'normal':

> If anything, the issue is more usefully posed the other way round. The conditions which made possible the formation of the modern psychological enterprise in England were established in all those fields where psychological expertise could be deployed in relation to problems of the abnormal functioning of individuals.
>
> *(Rose, 1985, p. 3)*

As a scientific enterprise, then, psychology sought to establish and define particular psychological and behavioral 'problems,' develop particular theories and methods to examine these 'problems,' and elicit particular forms of evidence and explanations to solve them. This enterprise was not merely descriptive but rather served as a powerful form of action, accomplishing the functional goals of European modernism and its brand of cultural imperialism (Spary, 1999). Here, psychology became a self-appointed arbiter of human behavior whose central role was to distinguish between conduct that did or did not require regulation within a binary framework of 'normality' and 'pathology.' Along these lines, contemporary formulations of the psychology of 'the individual' – and corresponding understandings of psychological phenomena – must be understood not as products of progressively more accurate scientific observations, but as products of a very specific program of institutional knowledge production:

> To understand the psychology of the individual in this light enables us to place its emergence as a scientific discourse, not within a history of reflections upon the nature of the soul, but within the changing conceptions of pathologies of thought, belief, intellect, emotion and conduct. It is to these conceptions and the practices of government, regulation, surveillance, segregation, and therapy within which they were deployed, that we must look if we are to begin to identify the conditions which made such a psychology possible.
>
> Not a history of ideas, then, but a history of practices, techniques, institutions and agencies, of the forms of knowledge which made them thinkable and which they, in their turn, transformed. And a history of the categories and problems around which such complex apparatuses formed, which provided the motivation for their emergence and the targets of their tactics. The feeble-minded individual, the shell-shocked soldier, the inefficient worker, the maladjusted child, the juvenile delinquent – no doubt these are simply the ones which have been most obvious in this particular study.
>
> *(Rose, 1985, p. 6)*

In the United States and Europe, mainstream trauma theory in the psy disciplines has become almost unequivocally informed by these formulations of individuated psychology (Fassin & Rechtman, 2009). Indeed, the *shell-shocked soldier* was a primary and "obvious" (Rose, 1985, p. 6) target of this individuated discipline at the time of its formation. Rarely is it recognized that other modes of knowing (and knowing about) trauma are available, and those who question dominant paradigms have been met with hostility (Fassin & Rechtman, 2009). Because the psy disciplines are so heavily dominated by this individuated framework, diverse knowledges have been cast as 'alternative' and explored largely *outside* of the psy disciplines (e.g., Alexander, 2012; Kurtz, 2018; Leys, 2000; Stevens, 2011). Subsequently, mainstream trauma theory comes from the histories, assumptions, and practices that underpin dominant psychological and psychiatric knowledge, while at the same time remaining largely devoid of (and resistant to) critical examination of these histories, assumptions, and practices.

A Medical Model of Trauma

The historical development of the psy disciplines along scientific lines aligned heavily with the medical model of the time. During the shift to modernism, the central role of naturalism led to the privileging of a 'Western' allopathic medical model within and beyond the realms of medicine (Spary, 1999). This included the psy disciplines (Scull, 2015). The classifications used by naturalists "slipped between the natural world and the social… to establish not only the expertise of the naturalists over the natural, but also the dominance of the natural over the social" (Spary, 1999, p. 281–2). This shift fundamentally drove the development of biological theories about – and responses to – socially situated experiences: psychological distress was interpreted as physical illness. The emphasis from the outset was on the medical interpretation of psychological phenomena, and psychiatrists largely worked as doctors in hospitals or asylums. This has been termed 'institutional psychiatry' (Scull, 2015). This discipline of psychiatry was formally institutionalized in the United States as the Association of Medical Superintendents of American Institutions for the Insane (AMSAII) in 1844, and the American Medico-Psychological Association in 1892, before becoming the American Psychiatric Association (APA) in 1921. The establishment of the APA was intertwined with the establishment of the American Medical Association (AMA), which was founded in 1847 in order to regulate medical licensing, education, and practice. These two institutions even shared a founder: physician and psychiatrist Pliny Earle II. Therefore, the institutions of psychiatry and medicine were inextricable from their very beginnings. Early debates in psychiatry reveal contested therapeutic claims, approaches, and conceptualizations of mental 'illness' and 'disorder' (e.g., Goodheart, 2016; Scull, 2015). Specifically, debates ensued over the moral and physical causes of insanity (Showalter, 1985), reflecting a struggle for epistemic dominance in the psy disciplines.

The expansion of private 'office-based psychiatry' after World War II reflected a broader expansion of the discipline of psychiatry in the United States (Scull, 2015). Dominated by psychoanalytic perspectives, this mode of psychiatry was gradually displaced by medical perspectives with more 'precise' classification and diagnostic systems, which were required by – and supported – a growing pharmaceutical industry (Scull, 2015). Contemporary biopsychiatry, informed by the dominant biomedical model, now promotes symptoms-based approaches that interpret psychological distress through a biomedical diagnostic framework (Lewis, 2011). This involves recording and classifying observed symptoms and then attempting to treat these symptoms as though they have an underlying physiological origin. These perspectives are informed by disease models of mental illness and have ultimately assumed such dominance in psychiatry that they have been criticized from within and outside of the discipline. For instance, China Mills' critical consideration of the biologization of psychiatry echoes earlier warnings from the former president of the American Psychiatric Association, Steven Sharfstein, that "we have allowed the bio-psycho-social model to become the bio-bio-bio model" (Cited in Mills, 2014, p. 33). These warnings came in response to the dominance of the biopsychiatric model and a proliferation of research and practice concerned with understanding only the biological dimensions and 'mechanisms' of psychological phenomena and distress. Here, biological phenomena tend to be presented as the ultimate explanatory 'factor' or 'trigger' for observed symptoms, leaving psychological and social domains untouched (Mills, 2014).

At the core of this 'psychiatric revolution' (Showalter, 1985) was an emphasis on rationalism that, by this time, had been firmly established as the preserve of privileged white men. Projected from a position of white selfhood, this pathologizing gaze brought everyone into the orbit of European and North American colonial dominance. For example, femininity was deemed irrational, unruly, and in need of regulation by rational masculinity (Haaken, 2021; Showalter, 1985; Tosh, 2016). This gaze also established essentialist biological constructs of race and class, which were in turn (re)produced by scientific theory and epistemology, including Social Darwinism, eugenics, criminology, and psychoanalysis (Stevens, 2011). Borrowing from the natural sciences, social scientific activity sought to establish systems of classification and, necessarily, difference on this basis. In the case of race, these systems were grounded in racial logics of "incommensurable difference" (Stevens, 2011, p. 182), producing a normative human subject in relation to an alienated Other. This Other was racialized and observed through logics of normative whiteness (Tosh & Carson, 2016), wherein whiteness constituted humanness. The racialized, dehumanized Other was, in comparison, deemed incapable of such wholeness; denied humanness and the capacity for suffering. This was accomplished through "naturalized ideas of racialized peoples as lacking the psychic interiority that could make psychic trauma, or even basic suffering, a social possibility" (Stevens, 2011, p. 182). The politics of this gaze are therefore visible not only in what or who came under its view, but also in what or who did not:

> Ultimately, the convergence of these ideas and their inherent logics conspired to exclude the experiences of racialized ethnic communities from the category of catastrophe that could be called traumatogenic.
> *(Stevens, 2011, p. 183)*

It is important to recognize that the histories and politics of this scientific enterprise constitute the present, which further debunks the narrative of 'objective' scientific study that dominates the psy disciplines. Indeed, it is not difficult to see how these histories constitute the epistemic and material ground on which understandings of trauma have been cultivated, and whose experiences, bodies, and lives matter in their realms. In recognition of this, I will now examine the two most dominant interpretative frameworks of trauma – *PTSD* and *neurobiology* – to consider where they come from and thus how 'trauma' became an object of institutional study and an outcome of institutional knowledge production. Specifically, I refer to these frameworks as *Trauma* ⇔ *PTSD* and *The Neurobiology of Trauma*.

Trauma ⇔ *PTSD*

The first dominant interpretation of trauma I will discuss was formalized through the diagnostic category of Post Traumatic Stress Disorder (PTSD) in 1980. This dominant interpretative framework casts trauma as synonymous with PTSD, and vice versa. Lodged in a biopsychiatric framework, the PTSD diagnosis introduced a clinical model of trauma, based on broader interpretations of psychological distress as a brain-based pathology or disease. Therefore, from the outset, the PTSD category defined trauma as psychopathological. Based on dominant notions of the individuated psychological subject, and arranged around the 'pole of abnormality' (Rose, 1985), trauma was imagined as an individual-level phenomenon requiring individual-level intervention. Here, the individual was identified as the site of trauma and its management.

PTSD characterized trauma via a series of symptoms, such as recurring memories, dreams, or flashbacks to a traumatic event, distress in response to reminders of a traumatic event, behavioral changes such as avoidance of thoughts or reminders of a traumatic event, and observed affective or cognitive changes such as mood changes, memory loss, fear, detachment, and distorted understandings of the traumatic event. This definition largely drew on notions of *subjective dissociation*, which originated and gained dominance via Freudian conceptualizations of trauma (Traverso & Broderick, 2010). From this perspective, trauma was conceptualized as an experience so catastrophic that it could not be assimilated into narrative memory via an individual's subjective assessment, existing instead in dissociated, unrepresentable, pathological memories beyond the realms of representation and control (Seeley, 2018). Critics have noted that subscribers to this concept have drawn on it to explain how "good people can do bad things" (Haaken, 2021, p. 58). In essence, it is argued, those 'bad things' occur in a dissociated state and therefore cannot be the fault of the inherently 'good' person. On this basis, the PTSD diagnosis has been used to justify a range of violent behaviors. For example, it has been invoked as a legal defense for murder and war crimes (Haaken, 2021).

The PTSD category originated in deliberations over *railway spine* following industrial accidents, and *shell shock* in military hospitals during World War I, which conceptualized trauma within the institutional realms of legalized, medicalized, and militarized discourses (Griffiths, 2018; Stevens, 2011; Thompson, 2021; Traverso & Broderick, 2010). This militarized status functioned to establish and bolster the authority of psychiatrists (Haaken, 2021). During this time, extensive military deliberations over *shell shock* located trauma as an illness to be cured in the interests of furthering the imperial war mission by (ideally) enabling soldiers to return to their military duties. However, this was made increasingly impossible by the growing phenomenon of 'battle fatigue' (Haaken, 2021). Since its origination, then, the PTSD category has been inextricably tied to militarized realms, eventually being formalized following advocacy to recognize the experiences of Vietnam War veterans. Therefore, its genealogy clearly locates PTSD as a specific conceptualization of trauma sustained in the line of military duty rather than a totalizing account of trauma. However, PTSD has been applied expansively and in a totalizing way to account for trauma *beyond* the confines of war. Indeed, most of the scientific research examining trauma in a range of settings uses the PTSD diagnosis as criteria for inclusion, and work carried out in the militarized domain has been extrapolated beyond these realms.

Within the context of military research, critical scholars have recognized that a medicalized model of trauma (and its treatment) may not be the most appropriate approach (Ali et al., 2020). However, this has yet to be critically considered or recognized in mainstream applications of the PTSD concept and category. Instead, based on the biopsychiatric model, there has been a push to conceptualize trauma primarily as a functional illness, and – on this basis – understand the ostensibly universal biological causes of PTSD and its associated symptoms. Trauma has also been defined as an antecedent to other forms of psychopathology (Rose, 2002). This knits trauma into a pathologizing net of 'risk factors' for 'comorbidities.' This net has been cast so wide that trauma is now associated almost universally with other forms of psychological distress.

Critical trauma theorists have recognized the specificity of PTSD as a dominant interpretative framework for trauma, referring to PTSD as "the diagnostic category used to describe symptomatic responses to trauma in relation to mental health" (Stevens, 2011, p. 175). This definition serves to distinguish the PTSD category as one specific and institutionally bound conceptualization of trauma. Echoing feminist arguments that 'the universal' is highly particular (e.g., Ahmed, 2007; Dean, 1996), this distinction has been made to illustrate that PTSD is in fact one very specific interpretation of trauma (Stevens, 2011). However, this definition "became the basis for all subsequent training and research in the field" (Leys, 2000, p. 232). Subsequently, PTSD has been consistently reproduced as *the* formal interpretation of trauma to the point that the two have become virtually synonymous. This is problematic, not least because there are many responses to events that would be considered traumatic that are not captured by PTSD diagnostic criteria. And, only a small proportion of people who experience what would be considered a traumatic event go on to develop what is referred to as PTSD. Additionally, it has been observed that PTSD diagnostic criteria give a narrow and insufficient delineation of the traumatic 'event' and its impacts, again limiting what it can account for (Stevens, 2011). Stevens notes the theoretical and practical shortcomings of this delineation:

> the location of trauma's origin can make it inaccessible to the PTSD model. This is apparent in the case of acute traumatic episodes originating in sociocultural structures where the traumatogenic agent is not readily discernable... Categories like ongoing or repeated trauma, multigenerational institutional relations, or even the sense of *impending* trauma that can produce PTSD symptoms, are all types of trauma that fall outside temporal parameters of conventionally applied models of injury.
>
> *(Stevens, 2011, p. 179)*

These shortcomings are not simply deficits of the PTSD model. Rather, just as what is *included* is present by design, what is *excluded* is absent by design. Indeed, "diagnoses are invented, not discovered" (Howell, 2012, p. 215). Viewed this way, the PTSD category can be viewed as an institutional accomplishment that has served to regulate knowledge(s) about trauma in specific ways, with tangible consequences. For this reason, Haaken (2021) draws attention to the powerful role of institutional knowledge in the discursive (re)production and regulation of 'trauma' via the PTSD category, centering this as a core critical concern:

> Critiques of psychiatry target its reliance on psychopharmacological remedies – an area that includes treatment for PTSD. But my interest in psychiatry centers on its powerful role in producing and regulating diagnostic categories.
>
> *(Haaken, 2021, p. 5)*

From this perspective, the PTSD diagnosis is not simply a descriptive label but a specific way of knowing about trauma that invites and accomplishes particular actions. This extends to scientific research, theory, teaching, clinical training, and even popular discourse.

The Neurobiology of Trauma

The second major dominant interpretation of trauma I will discuss is the *neurobiology of trauma*. In line with dominant biomedical frameworks, recent research and scholarship have prioritized a focus on neurobiological theories and explanations of trauma. Here, psychological life is understood through the prism of biological mechanics. Some of the most widely accepted and popular trauma theories argue that trauma is fundamentally 'etched' onto or stored within *The Body* via neurobiological mechanisms. These interpretations argue that the brain is essentially a biological organ of the body and should be viewed as such. These popular theories rely on "fixed notions of the body as text-to-be-read in a "realist" way" (Stevens, 2011, p. 175). I use the term '*The Body*' to recognize these assumptions. Specifically, I capitalize each word to emphasize the realist and universalized assumptions that presume there is one universal body – *The* body – that can be understood and accounted for in general terms, and that this *Body* can therefore be taken to represent all bodies. I italicize the term *The Body* to recognize the ubiquity of this term in popular trauma discourse.

Neurobiological discourses date back to the earliest accounts of trauma and now carry such epistemic currency that they are commonly viewed as the best explanation we have for trauma. In the first published account of a traumatic 'syndrome,' Erichsen (1866) argued – without biomedical evidence – that emotional trauma was a somatic symptom of physical injury (Stevens, 2011). This medical document was published in response to the expansion of the railway industry and the accidents and lawsuits this brought. Here, medicolegal discourse was fundamental to – and crystallized – renderings of a "*machinic* body whose ability to labor, or not, supplied the grounds for assessing damages" (Stevens, 2011, p. 174). This version of the body was central to and constructed specific interpretations of 'injury.' In the case of 'railway spine,' the injury in question was said to be directly located in and around the spinal cord. It is important to note that these interpretations were developed in order to *defend* railways against litigation. Thus, conceptualizations of the 'machinic' body were developed and served to protect corporate interests. The "postcatastrophe subject" (Stevens, 2011, p. 174) could then be diagnosed (or not) within this framework. This means that, from the outset, medicolegal discourse played a fundamental role in regulating what counted as trauma and what evidence indicated it. Notably, this gave physicians a special diagnostic prerogative, which allowed them to authorize or dismiss evidence of injury.

These assumptions ultimately evolved into contemporary mainstream neurobiological perspectives on trauma, and particularly the claim that trauma is 'stored' in *The Body*. From this perspective, trauma's occupation of the body causes particular physical symptoms. On this basis, it is argued, the body "signals the psychic truth of trauma" (Haaken, 2021, p. 100). This literal interpretation has been taken up by mainstream trauma theorists in dominant "medicalized portraits" of trauma (Haaken, 2021, p. 101). At the core of this argument lies the concept of a neurobiological "nexus of causality" between psychological distress and physiological response (Haaken, 2021, p. 100). Here, brain-based processes and specific brain regions are viewed as the architects of trauma. Thus, dominant neurobiological approaches imagine trauma primarily as an individual-level phenomenon and therefore focus on individual-level intervention. From this perspective, the individual is again identified as the site of trauma and its management.

It is important to note that such claims are not simply observations of universal fact but rather reflect specific epistemic claims with their own limitations and consequences. These specificities, limitations, and consequences are rarely acknowledged in dominant neurobiological discourse. For example, Ruth Leys (2000) famously examined widely promoted and enduring assumptions about the neurobiological bases of trauma in a critical analysis of *'The Science of the Literal.'* In this critique, Leys critically evaluated a large body of research that claims that trauma is "etched" into the brain (p. 239) and manifests in literal repetitions of traumatic events, such as nightmares, which are said to be exact replicas or "replays of the traumatic origin" (Leys, 2000, p. 233). According to these claims, traumatic nightmares are effectively an inflammatory response to neurobiological injury (Leys, 2000). In this conceptualization of trauma, inscribed into memory and expressed in reflex, the psychological subject is incapable of knowing their trauma without psychiatric intervention. Leys (2000) critically examined the epistemological and theoretical origins of these claims and the empirical evidence for them, and found limited support. For instance, she found that fundamental claims about the unique anatomy of traumatic nightmares were integrated into the APA's diagnostic classification of PTSD without empirical evidence, and that researchers "committed in advance" (Leys, 2000, p. 237) before retrospectively setting out to confirm such claims.

Leys (2000) notes that despite speculative disclaimers from the authors, these claims have been so widely cited in support of neurobiological theory that they have assumed an entrenched "appearance of solidity" (Leys, 2000, p. 239). Subsequently, assumptions that traumatic nightmares constitute "*literal memories* of the traumatic event" (Leys, 2000, p. 239) have become taken for granted to the point that they are rarely examined or questioned. Such literal interpretations also ignore the fact that memories "are neither stored nor parcelled out in discrete packages" (Seeley, 2018, p. 157). Rather, they are highly modulated and actively embodied through complex, plastic neural networks (Seeley, 2018). And, memories, understandings of events, and experiences are always bound up in affective and interpretative processes (Haaken, 1994; Seeley, 2018). This supports more recent calls for a conceptual shift in trauma theory from 'belated memories' to 'belated meanings' (Kruger, 2018). Others have argued that the very concepts of cognition and memory are a product of human and institutional knowledge production. In a series of arguments that reveal trauma as an object of institutional study, Stevens (2011) traces the institutional production and contingency of 'memory itself':

> Like trauma and memory itself, the *study* of memory and the formation of the memory sciences have a milieu and have taken their shape and cue from social contexts…
>
> … institutions that manage memory increasingly wear the robes of truth's arbiters… Its logics are those of the photograph or the gene or the eyewitness testimony; its functions converge to convey truth, to represent the real and to reproduce the Same… The science of memory has shifted from conceiving of its object, *memory*,

as an evolving entity open to processes of contestation, reframing, appropriation, diffraction, or simple dissolution, and has moved, again, with seeming inexorability, toward a focus on *history* as the fraught and always problematic recording of what has "gone on," as the recitation of actions and events contained within the past-perfect grammar of description, and the body's sometimes inaccurate keeping of the record.

(Stevens, 2011, p. 180)

There are also problems with the broader conceptualization of *The Body* that is said to record, or 'keep score' of, what has "gone on" (Stevens, 2011, p. 180). As discussed, broader notions of *The Body* are problematic because they support realist assumptions that there is one universal body, and that this *Body* can be taken to represent all bodies. Such universalized conceptualizations account for *The Body* as though it is simply a biological artifact. In this sense, dominant claims about the bodily nature of trauma function to essentialize trauma. One problem with this type of explanation is that it is usually accompanied by a failure to recognize that biological knowledge is socially constructed and embedded: that the biological artifact of *The Body* itself is a human creation (Tosh, 2020). Another problem is that universalized notions of *The Body* are in fact quite specific and refer to a typical body; more specifically, a *neuro*typical body. Indeed, most trauma theorizing presumes a universal, prototypical body, characterized by 'standard' physiological and neurobiological processes and responses. This 'standard' body is defined by the parameters of neurotypicality and therefore saturated with ableist assumptions. This is rarely acknowledged in broader discourses and responses to trauma.

Despite these specificities and limitations, neurobiological interpretations of trauma have ascended to the status of truth in trauma discourse, which fundamentally constrains how trauma can be known and known about. By conceptualizing the brain primarily as a bodily organ, these interpretations fix the scope of what can be understood about trauma and limit possibilities to imagine trauma otherwise (Stevens, 2011). Indeed, while neurobiology is implicated in every aspect of human experience, neurobiological explanations alone cannot account for the entirety, complexity, richness, and diversity of psychological experiences. This has been recognized by those in the discipline of the philosophy of neuroscience (e.g., Bennett & Hacker, 2022), who also recognize that neurobiology does not simply boil down to a split between brain-based (mechanical; biological) and mind-based (non-mechanical; psychological) properties, where brain-based properties can or should be isolated. In addition, as Haaken (2021) argues, dominant neurobiological perspectives cannot fully account for the causal 'nexus' between psychological distress and physiological response:

> Physical symptoms do not directly reveal underlying causes. The body registers distress through physiological processes, but not in a way that translates to a straightforward nexus of causality.
> *(Haaken, 2021, p. 100)*

Therefore, while *biological* theory and research constitute one area of psychological exploration, this should not subsume a range of related areas of *psychological* exploration. Such considerations are not well integrated into contemporary popular trauma discourse, meaning that universalized 'brain claims' are often circulated uncritically in a broad spectrum of scholarly work with very little critical consideration of their validity or explanatory relevance to complex social issues (Tseris, 2019). One major consequence of this is that dominant neurobiological explanations have obscured a range of possibilities for imagining and understanding trauma.

As Tseris (2019) observes, the contemporary captivation with neurobiological explanations of trauma can be explained as a consequence of *neuroenchantment*, which refers to "a form of sub-judicious fascination with brain science" (Ali et al., 2014, p. 1). This is characterized by an individual and cultural tendency to assign credibility or merit to anything resembling neuroscience and a tendency to overestimate the explanatory value and power of neuroscience on this basis. For example, in their highly creative research, Ali et al. found that students in the psy disciplines uncritically accepted the legitimacy of a brain scanner that was apparently trained in mind-reading, despite having learned that mind-reading is impossible, and despite the use of an "absurd and ramshackle" 'brain scanner' made of "glorified hair-dryer apparatus" (p. 3). This is coupled with rising "neuroimaging hype" and the academic practice of "spicing up arguments with the rhetorical accoutrements of neuroscience" (Ali et al., 2014, p. 1). It is easy to see how, under these conditions, neurobiological explanations of trauma have become dominant at the expense of other explanations or areas of focus: their supporting evidence is inaccessible to a large proportion of people, and such explanations carry a great deal of currency and allure, especially when endorsed by psychological and scientific 'experts.' This has bolstered dominant perspectives, prioritizing a focus on individual-level explanations and interpretations at the expense of others.

Critical and Feminist Psychological Responses to Dominant Euro-American Conceptualizations of Trauma

The analyses presented thus far show how 'trauma' has become an object of institutional study and an outcome of institutional knowledge production. In line with the first principle of feminist psychology outlined by Burman (1992) in Chapter 1, this analysis has been concerned with the specificities and contingencies of dominant conceptualizations of trauma, and how they reflect certain assumptions or interests. Such analyses show that what is *meant* by trauma in any given time and place is not all that is or can be *known* about trauma. Rather, it is a specific representation of trauma reflecting (and privileging) particular ways of 'Knowing' (Liebert, 2019). For instance, dominant Euro-American conceptualizations focus on identifying fundamental components or mechanisms of trauma in individuals. In keeping with modernist traditions, this relies on and reproduces the concept of the self-contained individual and reduces trauma to internal features and processes within the individual. Here, the individual is imagined in isolation from the socio-political conditions that underpin their experiences.

Against dominant contemporary conceptualizations of trauma, it can be difficult to imagine trauma otherwise. Such interpretations operate with the kind of certainty adopted by the mainstream psy disciplines in their pursuit of scientific credibility (Tseris, 2013). A critical focus on these interpretations is important, especially because the concept of trauma employed in mental health-related settings remains largely tied to dominant models of individual pathology (Tseris, 2019). This concern is not simply the preserve of critical feminist academics. Indeed, those working in mental health-related settings have also expressed concern over the "under-examined implications" of dominant biological and neuroscientific paradigms in this space (Tseris, 2019, p. 4). To synthesize this analysis, I will now turn to Burman's remaining feminist psychological principles to render the 'truth' claims of dominant conceptualizations of trauma problematic and reframe universalizing claims as socially constituted and provisional. I will also propose an epistemic reorientation that views trauma knowledge as discursively produced and associated with specific forms of regulation (Burman, 1992). Here, I will invoke critical and feminist psychological perspectives to reveal the institutional specificities of dominant conceptualizations of trauma. On this basis, I will then define *institutional trauma* in the first sense: as an object of institutional knowledge (and knowledge production).

Feminist readings situate trauma as a socially constituted and provisional concept (e.g., Tseris, 2019). Trauma, and the medicalized discourses that coalesce around it, are viewed from this perspective as culturally and historically specific and situated (Tseris, 2019). This can be seen in the earliest forms of psychiatric deliberation over trauma in accounts of *railway spine* and *shell shock*, through to the age of *neuroenchantment*. As discussed in this chapter, these accounts were never neutral, instead reflecting a range of interests. As such, Stevens (2011) argues that 'trauma' can be understood as a cultural object:

> Rather than thinking of trauma as an identifiable and discrete event that must have occurred at some specific point in time and place, it can be framed as a cultural object whose meanings far exceed the boundaries of any particular shock or disruption.
> *(Stevens, 2011, p. 179)*

In response, feminist psychologists have identified trauma as a culturally contingent and specific object, calling into question the philosophical assumptions, histories, and applications of dominant conceptualizations. This is based on the critical feminist psychological observation that knowledge is always socio-historically located, specific, and contingent. For instance, in her conceptualization of 'trauma talk,' Jeanne Marecek articulates trauma as a culturally situated object of knowledge and practice. Marecek (1999) defines trauma talk as a "lexicon" or "system of terms, metaphors, and modes of representation" (p. 158–159) for talking about physical and sexual abuse. Here, she takes a critical feminist psychological approach to show how language, discourse, and power fundamentally drive everyday meanings and knowledge production about trauma. In doing so, she argues that language functions to give trauma its meaning:

> language is not a transparent medium through which reality can be seen; rather, language creates the reality of which we speak. Language practices shape what we can see and think. Moreover, language is not a vehicle for expressing private thoughts formulated inside a speaker's head; it is a social practice. Trauma, with all its attributes and associations, exists by virtue of cultural agreements to package it in this particular way.
> *(Marecek, 1999, p. 159)*

In this work, Marecek examined how 'trauma talk' operated in feminist therapists' accounts of therapeutic practice. Here, she identified a particular 'vocabulary of distress,' grounded in the conflation of trauma and

PTSD, "consisting of terms such as *trauma, wound, injury, emotional pain, brokenness*, and *damage*, to describe clients' problems" (Marecek, 1999, p. 162). One particularly problematic component of this lexicon was that PTSD was not critically interrogated or problematized in the same way that other diagnostic categories were. Therapists also drew on physical metaphors and explanations to explain trauma, relying on heavily individualized and medicalized concepts. This meant that "far from countering the medicalized idiom of conventional psychiatry, [trauma talk] has merely replaced one form of this idiom with another" (Marecek, 1999, p. 165). As such, Marecek shows how trauma talk functions to "construct clinical realities" (p. 177), therefore bringing implications for practice. In doing so, she argues that "psychology's habits of authoritative expertise and its claim of privileged access to a single Truth, even when practiced in the name of feminism, should be received with skepticism" (Marecek, 1999, p. 180).

Subsequent feminist psychological work has also shown how dominant biomedical frameworks powerfully shape how people understand trauma more broadly (Gavey & Schmidt, 2011). This work has demonstrated that dominant meanings are not merely descriptive but instead profoundly shape the possibilities for understanding and action in response to trauma. In this study, Gavey and Schmidt (2011) explored the frameworks of meaning that groups of 'lay' participants drew on when discussing the impacts of rape. This work showed how participants constructed a dominant *trauma of rape* discourse grounded in the fundamental assumptions of dominant interpretative frameworks. Here, participants constructed trauma primarily as an individual psychological phenomenon and as a permanent 'scar' etched into the body (Gavey & Schmidt, 2011). This discourse drew directly on dominant neurobiological interpretations of trauma. However, rape was also considered to be so traumatic that an absence of this kind of traumatic response was constructed as pathological (Gavey & Schmidt, 2011). For example, participants argued that those who did not express this kind of traumatic response were in denial (Gavey & Schmidt, 2011). This served to position those who did not express trauma in the 'appropriate' way as being out of touch with psychological reality, and even in danger (Gavey & Schmidt, 2011). Such discourses reveal the power of such dominant interpretative frameworks to regulate 'appropriate' expressions of trauma.

The authors also argue that while participants expressed 'sympathetic' perspectives on trauma and shifted away from dismissive responses to rape, their accounts still carried "double-edged—and not *entirely* helpful—implications" (Gavey & Schmidt, 2011, p. 449). For instance, the authors observed a "swing" from the dismissive universalizing presumption that "no harm is done" to another universalizing presumption that "severe harm is done" (Gavey & Schmidt, 2011, p. 449). The 'catastrophic logics' (Stevens, 2011) underpinning such interpretations will be discussed further in Chapter 3, but one of the main 'effects' of such logics is an urgent cultural imperative to 'fix' trauma in appropriate ways, which is typically leveled at the individual psychological subject in line with biopsychiatric approaches. This research therefore provides an example of how dominant interpretations of trauma are socially constituted and (re)produced, and what forms of response and action they privilege over others. As such, the authors argue that dominant meanings and conceptualizations of trauma carry substantial social and political 'effects.' For instance, they observe that dominant conceptualizations and their 'prescriptive absolutes' reproduce "the reductive, prescriptive, and depoliticizing potential of increasingly medicalized and psychologized ways of understanding the impact of sexual violence" (Gavey & Schmidt, 2011, p. 449). Thus, in line with the principles of feminist psychology, the authors call for an epistemic reorientation to understand violence and its impacts beyond such absolutes, in the recognition that this is both produced and constrained by powerful interpretative frameworks and discourses. This brings us to the definition of *institutional trauma* in the first sense, where trauma is understood as an object of institutional knowledge (and knowledge production).

Institutional Trauma: **Trauma as an Object of Institutional Knowledge (and Knowledge Production)**

In relation to trauma, critical trauma theorists have responded to calls for epistemic change most clearly, offering an epistemic reorientation that views trauma knowledge as institutionally produced. Scholars in the domain of critical trauma studies argue that meanings about trauma are socially and historically contingent and laden with institutional concerns and interests. This orientation recognizes the profound entanglement of institutions and trauma, based on the observation that conceptualizations and interpretations of trauma are institutionally bound and produced. As such, trauma is conceptualized not simply as a descriptive label applied to certain observed behaviors. Rather, conceptualizations of trauma are viewed as institutional accomplishments that function to define trauma and traumatized subjects in very specific ways. This profoundly impacts how trauma can be understood and addressed. As such, it has been observed that "trauma does not simply describe subjects and/

or their embodied experiences, it also, and perhaps more accurately, *creates* them" (Stevens, 2011, p. 178).

As Stevens observes:

> notions of trauma emerge as often very complex "sets of practice" in several cultural institutions... namely, the clinic, legal discourse, cyberspace, popular culture, and, of course, the street.
> *(Stevens, 2011, p. 177)*

Here, it is argued that meanings about trauma vary and produce a range of 'social effects' (Stevens, 2011). This critical approach to trauma considers the specific and provisional status of such meanings and their effects in terms of their consequences and the interests they serve:

> "Trauma" circulates among various social contexts that give it differing meanings and coproduce its multiple social effects, and its component memes, those pivotal conceptualizations that tailor its function, have origins that can be traced to coordinates that vary in time, space, and semiosis; coordinates whose ideological concerns come to refract or anchor trauma's meanings in very fixed notions of the body and our sense of embodiment.
> *(Stevens, 2011, p. 179–180)*

This institutional orientation also reveals the functions of such meanings by showing how dominant forms of knowledge are associated with specific forms of regulation. Indeed, Stevens (2011) argues that the concept of trauma has been contested and shifting since the late 19th century due to its regulatory functions in litigation contexts:

> In fact, from its first applications in the explanation of symptoms deriving from railway accidents, trauma has really never functioned transparently or equitably and has never been an unencumbered descriptive term. For as soon as victims began making claims on their injuries, as soon, that is, as the *harm* attending this particular form of industrial movement had its place in the lexicon of litigation, insurance agents working in the service of railway companies, and the surgeons in their employ, began defining who could and who could not be understood as having been traumatized and just what the nature of apparently nonsomatic injury might be. These were *scientific* determinations that fell then, as they do now, along axes marked by *cultural* categories of social differentiation; and that rose, as they

often do, buoyed on the thermals of emergent technologies of medical detection and medicolegal reasoning.

(Stevens, 2011, p. 173)

Stevens (2011) also argues that this concept of trauma was "racialized, sexualized, gendered, and classed from its inception" (p. 173), which allowed physicians to determine "who could and who could not be understood as having been traumatized" (p. 173). Such observations lend themselves to intersectional analysis by allowing for considerations of who is rendered legible and who is rendered illegible by particular forms of knowledge and practice (Cooper, 2015). In the case of trauma, dominant constructions of trauma sustained in military service contributed to a narrow view of what trauma was and who could experience it. This view on trauma, established through clinical practice, functioned to define trauma in relation to the normative standards of whiteness and uphold established power:

> Because the traumatized subject has been one constructed through medical, psychological, legal, academic, and cultural institutions that are themselves based on racially unmarked subjects/bodies, it makes sense to understand both the subject of trauma and trauma itself to be similarly unmarked, and framed in terms of a body that is "essentially" white.
>
> *(Stevens, 2011, p. 183)*

Taking the example of the PTSD diagnosis and its "enabling agents (clinics, clinicians, psychotropics, therapies, institutional recognitions, bodily performances, etc.)" (p. 183), Stevens (2011) conceptualizes PTSD as "a bundle of social practices that reflect how trauma is invoked in clinical/medical institutions" (p. 183). On this basis, Stevens argues that such institutional practices produce 'legible subjects' whose behaviors register with institutional conceptualizations: "that is, he or she who has been traumatized and is exhibiting symptoms that warrant the diagnostic categorization of PTSD and the disciplinary practices that spring into action in the application of the diagnosis" (p. 183), marking out who could become legible as traumatized – and traumatizable – within such a view. Such an analysis shows how, in privileging biopsychiatric models, dominant disciplines brought only some forms of trauma into view in line with established power. Indeed, as Stevens observes, medical models operated via the logics of white supremacy to deny the trauma of racialization and its consequences. Further still, by casting the racialized 'Other' as untraumatizable, white supremacist logics – driven by the principles of dehumanization – denied this racialized 'Other' the capacity to be traumatized, rendering them devoid of the 'psychic interiority' needed to make them legible:

> From Freud, Darwin, and the scientific racisms of the nineteenth and twentieth centuries, to the postpleasurable traumas of World War II and the recuperative practices of American clinical psychology and neurobiology, psychoanalytic theories and psychotherapeutic practices have been unable to take up racialization as a social process that produces some subjects as vulnerable to traumatogenic injury, and others as not. Indeed, the "Others" to this village of the traumatizable, because they are the ultimate source of phobia and, therefore, cannot be overwhelmed by it, are not imagined to possess the psychic interiority necessary for identification and institutional legibility.
> *(Stevens, 2011, p. 182)*

As such, dominant biopsychiatric conceptualizations of trauma represent a "formation of ideas about whose sensibilities or fragile connections can be disturbed by near-death experiences, whose civility can be upset by the horrific, and who can be overwhelmed by fear; who or what, in short, can be traumatized" (Stevens, 2011, p. 177). Given the origins of such dominant frameworks, these observations resonate with Puleng Segalo's argument that the dominant Euro-American trauma concept is a "neo-colonial imposition" that functions to marginalize and silence localized understandings and responses to distress (Segalo, 2015, p. 447). Extending this argument, the dominant Euro-American trauma concept can, then, also be understood as a neo-colonial imposition that functions to define what can be viewed as distress and who can be viewed as distressed.

Conclusion

In contrast with the *negative space* of institutions, dominant biopsychiatric conceptualizations of trauma stand out in the foreground; their shape and meaning imparted by institutions that are never recognized as such. An institutional analytic brings this contrast into view, showing how "trauma, as a situated knowledge that emerges from the specificities of the moment in which it is invoked as an appropriate or obvious label, bears in rather remarkable ways, traces that reveal its cultural work" (Stevens, 2011, p. 176). An institutional analytic of trauma defines trauma in the first sense as a situated knowledge, moving beyond notions of trauma as a diagnostic category or biological artifact. Viewing such interpretations as limited, this institutional reorientation imagines trauma otherwise to promote institutional understandings and responses to trauma. Here, trauma is imagined as an institutional phenomenon:

> Shifting from our conception of trauma as a descriptive term, and moving to thinking of it as a concept that makes subjects and shapes bodies through the function of significant social institutions, can help us determine and propose alternative approaches to assessing and responding to our social suffering...
>
> *(Stevens, 2011, p. 185)*

In line with this institutional analytic, it is therefore important to consider the assumptions and definitions at play in any invocation of trauma, the work these assumptions and definitions are doing, and the responses they invite. This is specifically important because dominant assumptions and definitions of trauma inform a wide range of cultural practices and responses. In Chapter 3, I will examine the institutional practices that bring these dominant knowledge(s) and conceptualizations of trauma to bear. In doing so, I will show how these dominant frameworks inform *prescriptive logics*, which set out specific instructions for how trauma should be addressed. I will argue on this basis that an institutional analytic is especially necessary to understand these practices, their logics, and their consequences.

References

Ahmed, S. (2007). A phenomenology of whiteness. *Feminist Theory*, 8(2), 149–167. https://doi.org/10.1177/1464700107078139

Alexander, J. C. (2012). *Trauma: A Social Theory*. Polity Press.

Ali, A., Wolfert, S., McGovern, J. E., Nguyen, J., & Aharoni, A. (2020). A trauma-informed analysis of monologues constructed by military veterans in a theater-based treatment program. *Qualitative Research in Psychology*, 17(2), 258–273. https://doi.org/10.1080/14780887.2018.1442704

Ali, S. S., Lifshitz, M., & Raz, A. (2014). Empirical neuroenchantment: From reading minds to thinking critically. *Frontiers in Human Neuroscience*, 8(MAY). https://doi.org/10.3389/fnhum.2014.00357

Bennett, M. R., & Hacker, P. M. S. (2022). *Philosophical Foundations of Neuroscience* (2nd ed.). Wiley-Blackwell.

Burman, E. (1992). Feminism and discourse in developmental psychology: Power, subjectivity and interpretation. *Feminism & Psychology*, 2(1), 45–59.

Canguilhem, G. (1978). *On The Normal and the Pathological* (C. R. Fawcett, Trans.). D. Reidel Publishing Company.

Cooper, B. (2015). Intersectionality. In L. J. Disch & M. E. Hawkesworth (Eds.), *The Oxford Handbook of Feminist Theory* (pp. 385–406). Oxford University Press.

Dean, J. (1996). *Solidarity of Strangers: Feminism after Identity Politics*. University of California Press.
Erichsen, J. E. (1866). *On Railway and Other Injuries of the Nervous System*. Walton and Maberly.
Fassin, D., & Rechtman, R. (2009). *The Empire of Trauma*. Princeton University Press.
Gavey, N., & Schmidt, J. (2011). "Trauma of rape" discourse: A double-edged template for everyday understandings of the impact of rape? *Violence Against Women*, 17(4), 433–456. https://doi.org/10.1177/1077801211404194
Gone, J. P. (2008). Introduction: Mental health discourse as western cultural proselytization. *Ethos*, 36(3), 310–315. https://doi.org/10.1111/j.1548-1352.2008.00016.x
Goodheart, L. (2016). "The glamour of arabic numbers": Pliny earle's challenge to nineteenth-century psychiatry. *Journal of the History of Medicine and Allied Sciences*, 71(2), 173–196. https://doi.org/10.1093/jhmas/jrv022
Griffiths, J. (2018). Feminist Interventions in Trauma Studies. In J. R. Kurtz (Ed.), *Trauma and Literature* (pp. 181–195). Cambridge University Press.
Haaken, J. (1994). Sexual abuse, recovered memory, and therapeutic practice: A feminist-psychoanalytic perspective. *Social Text*, 40, 115–145. https://www.jstor.org/stable/466798?seq=1&cid=pdf-
Haaken, J. (2021). *Psychiatry, Politics, and PTSD: Breaking Down*. Routledge.
Howell, A. (2012). The demise of PTSD: From governing through trauma to governing resilience. *Alternatives*, 37(3), 214–226. https://doi.org/10.1177/0304375412450842
Khúc, M. (2024). *Dear Elia: Letters from the Asian American Abyss*. Duke University Press.
Kruger, M. (2018). Trauma and the Visual Arts. In J. R. Kurtz (Ed.), *Trauma and Literature* (pp. 255–269). Cambridge University Press.
Kurtz, J. R. (2018). *Trauma and Literature*. Cambridge University Press.
Lewis, B. (2011). *Narrative Psychiatry: How Stories Can Shape Clinical Practice*. Johns Hopkins University Press.
Leys, R. (2000). *Trauma: A Genealogy*. The University of Chicago Press.
Liebert, R. J. (2019). *Psycurity*. Routledge.
Marecek, J. (1999). Trauma Talk in Feminist Clinical Practice. In S. Lamb (Ed.), *New Versions of Victims: Feminists Struggle with the Concept* (pp. 158–182). New York University Press.
Mills, C. (2014). *Decolonizing Global Mental Health: The Psychiatrization of the Majority World*. Routledge.
Rose, N. (1985). *The Psychological Complex: Psychology, Politics and Society in England, 1869–1939*. Routledge & Kegan Paul.
Rose, S. (2002). Theoretical approaches to psychological trauma: Implications for research and practice. *Counselling and Psychotherapy Research*, 2(1), 61–72. https://doi.org/10.1080/14733140212331384998
Scull, A. (2015). *Madness in Civilization: A Cultural History of Insanity from the Bible to Freud, from the Madhouse to Modern Medicine*. Princeton University Press.
Seeley, W. P. (2018). Neuroscience, Narrative, and Emotion Regulation. In J. R. Kurtz (Ed.), *Trauma and Literature* (pp. 153–166). Cambridge University Press.

Segalo, P. (2015). Trauma and gender. *Social and Personality Psychology Compass*, 9(9), 447–454. https://doi.org/10.1111/spc3.12192

Showalter, E. (1985). *The Female Malady: Women, Madness and English Culture, 1830–1980*. Penguin Books Ltd.

Spary, E. (1999). The 'Nature' of Enlightenment. In W. Clark, S. Schaffer, & J. Golinski (Eds.), *The Sciences in Enlightened Europe* (pp. 272–304). University of Chicago Press.

Spivak, G. C. (1988). Can the Subaltern Speak? In C. Nelson & L. Grossberg (Eds.), *Marxism and the Interpretation of Culture* (pp. 271–313). University of Illinois Press.

Stevens, M. E. (2011). Trauma's Essential Bodies. In M. J. Casper & P. Currah (Eds.), *Corpus: An Interdisciplinary Reader on Bodies and Knowledge* (pp. 171–186). Palgrave Macmillan.

Thompson, L. (2021). Toward a feminist psychological theory of "institutional trauma." *Feminism & Psychology*, 31(1), 99–118. https://doi.org/10.1177/0959353520968374

Tosh, J. (2016). *Psychology and Gender Dysphoria: Feminist and Transgender Perspectives*. Routledge.

Tosh, J. (2020). *The Body and Consent in Psychology, Psychiatry, and Medicine: A Therapeutic Rape Culture*. Routledge.

Tosh, J., & Carson, K. (2016). A Desire to be "normal"? A discursive and intersectional analysis of "penetration disorder." *Intersectionalities: A Global Journal*, 5(3), 151–172.

Traverso, A., & Broderick, M. (2010). Interrogating trauma: Towards a critical trauma studies. *Continuum*, 24(1), 3–15. https://doi.org/10.1080/10304310903461270

Tseris, E. (2013). Trauma theory without feminism? evaluating contemporary understandings of traumatized women. *Affilia - Journal of Women and Social Work*, 28(2), 153–164. https://doi.org/10.1177/0886109913485707

Tseris, E. (2019). *Trauma, Women's Mental Health, and Social Justice: Pitfalls and Possibilities*. Routledge.

3
TRAUMA CAPITALISM

In Chapter 2, I argued that dominant conceptualizations and interpretations of trauma are not simply descriptive, but instead function to construct trauma and traumatized subjects in particular ways through particular sets of knowledge(s). Having examined dominant conceptualizations of trauma, in this chapter I will examine the institutional practices that bring these to bear. In doing so, I will argue that dominant conceptualizations of trauma provide *prescriptive logics*, which set out specific instructions for how trauma should be understood and addressed. I will begin with an examination of the broad institutional practices of psychiatrization (e.g., Mills, 2014; Rose, 2019), pathologization (e.g., Parker et al., 1995), and privatization (Thompson, 2021). I will then consider how these practices constitute and encourage *diagnostic imperialism* (Rose, 2019), which supports what has been referred to as the 'trauma industry' (Afuape, 2011). Next, I will examine the trauma industry and how this regulates experiences of – and responses to – trauma. Here, I will argue that the trauma industry is an expression of what I will call *trauma capitalism*: a set of socio-political and economic relations that leverage trauma in the interests of capitalism. In the last part of this chapter, I will consider the consequences and implications of trauma capitalism from feminist and critical psychological perspectives, with a specific focus on how this generates cultures of resilience, silence, and recovery.

Psychiatrization of Trauma

In line with the broader individualized and medicalized approach of the psy disciplines discussed in Chapter 2, dominant conceptualizations of trauma typically invite individualized and medicalized therapeutic responses informed by psychiatric frameworks. Here, it is assumed that psychic distress is caused by a pathology within the individual, which

DOI: 10.4324/9781003042471-3

can be diagnosed, treated, and cured with designated psychotherapeutic techniques (Kaye, 1999). Trauma is an archetypal example of this kind of interpretation. From this approach, trauma is understood primarily as a psychiatric concern. The practice of framing human distress as a psychiatric concern is referred to as *psychiatrization* (Mills, 2014). Psychiatrization relies on the broader practice of *psychologization*, which casts suffering and adversity into psychological frameworks and notions of the individual (Burr & Butt, 2000). In dominant trauma-informed frameworks, trauma is both defined and addressed through the practice of psychiatrization. For example, dominant trauma knowledges assert that trauma can primarily be observed and defined through specific sets of observable symptoms. This assertion is so powerful that it has subsumed other ways of knowing about trauma:

> The logics of trauma state that while its immensity renders its representation impossible, its traces in the form of symptoms inscribed on the body or in anomalies in the signification of embodiment, guarantee that an event actually took place. The symptoms we can observe and tick off our diagnostic list, the scars we can delicately trace with exploring eyes or fingers, the landscape whose barren patches we can lament, these are all signs in the here/now that assure the facticity of an event in the there/then.
> *(Stevens, 2011, p. 175–176)*

Consequently, dominant trauma knowledges render trauma unknowable outside of collections of symptoms and prescribe responses accordingly. Stevens (2011) argues that these dominant knowledges are largely underpinned by catastrophic logics, which create urgent calls to 'fix' the symptoms of trauma. Here, the individual serves as both the site of trauma and its management: They are broken and must be fixed. Without action, it is warned that trauma will languish in the body, wreaking havoc in one's life and relationships. Such logics construct an imperative to fix the problem, but to do so in 'appropriate' ways. This tightly regulates how trauma can be addressed. For example, 'appropriate' solutions are typically aligned with the assumptions and practices of Euro-American psychiatric perspectives on trauma (Gone, 2023). And, because dominant logics construct trauma as a problem within the individual, 'appropriate' solutions are typically focused on personal transformation.

Typical interventions for trauma in the psy disciplines focus on treating individual symptoms with private one-on-one counseling and therapies, medications, or a combination of both. Trauma-informed practitioners more broadly focus on addressing individual-level impacts and 'symptoms,' such as anxiety and emotional dysregulation, cognitive 'triggers,' and physical health. The ultimate goal of these efforts is to intervene in the 'effects' of trauma and bring the individual to a place of resilience and wellness. However, very little attention is paid to intervening in the conditions surrounding the experience of trauma. For this reason, it has been argued that psychiatrization transforms socially situated experiences of distress into individual problems to be solved at an individual level (Tseris, 2019). This diverts attention away from the socio-cultural conditions that give rise to and perpetuate distress (Kaye, 1999), and pulls trauma into the realms of the psy disciplines where trauma is constructed as maladaptive and pathological. Feminist psychologists have argued on this basis that psychiatrization fundamentally serves to pathologize suffering arising from socio-cultural conditions, with a specific focus on power and oppression:

> Understanding the experiences of depression or the trauma of rape, for example, as solely medical conditions, constructs women's suffering as individual pathology rather than a response to social injustice.
>
> *(McKenzie-Mohr & Lafrance, 2011, p. 50)*

Psychiatrization, then, is intimately connected with the pathologization of trauma.

Pathologization of Trauma

Pathologization refers to the institutional practice of constructing the 'abnormal' individual through the lens and power of the psy complex (Parker et al., 1995). Pathologization relies on psychiatrization through its construction of the individual in psychiatric terms. The construction of the 'abnormal' in the psy disciplines is centrally accomplished through the classification and diagnosis of psychiatric disorders. The *Diagnostic Statistical Manual of Mental Disorders*, a publication of the APA (e.g., American Psychiatric Association, 2022), defines and guides such classificatory and diagnostic practices, containing "everything that can possibly be wrong with a human being" (Kriss, 2013, para 4). As discussed in Chapter 2, this way of understanding psychological distress around the "pole of abnormality" (Rose, 1985, p. 5) serves regulative functions. For example, in the case of trauma, the psy complex places a firm focus on addressing the individual-level pathologies of symptoms and their outcomes, such as hypervigilance, anxiety, depression, and associated physiological processes, using medicalized and pharmaceutical interventions.

The most prolific and best-selling books on the topic of trauma are written by medical doctors, who are revered as 'gurus' on the subject. These books often make claims that are not supported by the evidence presented, which can inform practice in detrimental ways. Nietfeld (2025) highlights such issues in a critical analysis of one of the most popular books ever written about trauma, which I intentionally do not cite (for an extensive discussion of citation as a political practice, see Ahmed, 2017). In this critical analysis, Nietfeld (2025) identifies a litany of problems with this book's content, including speculation, victim blaming, misogyny, shaming and disgust, "appalling examples" (para. 31), pathologization, dehumanization, stigmatization, sweeping generalizations, de-politicizations of violence, and accounts of sexual violence that cast indigenous people as disposable for the sake of narratives that center white men. There is also the issue with the book's mischaracterization of evidence and inaccurate conclusions, which Nietfeld (2025) documents in collaboration with the cited authors. One broader issue, though, is that most of the best-selling books on trauma are written by privileged men from the dominant psychiatric perspective, and typically uncritically reproduce dominant de-politicized psychiatric concepts of trauma. For instance, while these books may concede that traditional pharmaceutical interventions may not suit all patients, the medicalized approach is still the default epistemological modus operandi for this genre and even underpins alternate treatment suggestions for patients, such as neurofeedback techniques and psychedelic pharmaceutical interventions. This "flattens violence into 'trauma,' ignoring the social forces that allow it to flourish" (Nietfeld, 2025, para 15).

It is also especially important to note, more broadly, that the diagnostic classifications taken in these best-selling books to mean biological reality are not informed by, and do not describe or provide, comprehensive evidence of biological pathologies (Bonanno, 2021). Rather, diagnostic categories describe expressed behaviors that are interpreted as symptoms of some underlying pathology:

> Just as Borges's system groups animals by seemingly aleatory characteristics entirely divorced from their actual biological attributes, DSM-5 arranges its various strains of madness solely in terms of the behaviors exhibited... ... while any consideration of the mind itself is entirely absent.
>
> *(Kriss, 2013, para 5)*

The conflation of expressed behaviors with underlying pathology places an even tighter grip on how such behaviors can be interpreted: rather than interpreting expressed behaviors or 'symptoms' as responses to social and relational conditions or moral injury, they are attributed to matters of biology. It is important to note two interrelated problems here. First, scientific claims about trauma from the psy disciplines rely on limited and often speculative evidence, but are presented as the 'truth' of trauma. Second, the dominance of these scientific claims obscures the institutionally bound conditions and relations that (a) give rise to scientific claims and their dominance, (b) shape how trauma is experienced, and (c) obscure the institutional contingency of these. It is also important to note that in raising these problems, the goal is not necessarily to dismiss scientific paradigms outright, but rather to question the legitimacy, dominance, and consequences of scientific claims about trauma, including pathologization.

Feminist psychologists have critiqued the pathologization of symptoms associated with trauma on the grounds that such symptoms are inextricable from the relations and conditions in which they arise. For example, in their work examining women's everyday acts of resistance against intimate partner violence (IPV), Black et al. (2020) observe that chronic anxiety is a rational and functional (as opposed to irrational and dysfunctional) response to persistently dangerous situations. They argue on this basis that "rather than pathologising women for this state of hypervigilance, our analysis points to the protective role such an embodied understanding of IPV can have in their lives" (p. 545). This (re)interpretation of pathologization understands 'symptoms' as active and adaptive responses to broader oppressive and dangerous conditions. More broadly, McKenzie-Mohr and Lafrance (2011, p. 52) critique dominant pathologizing responses to trauma, arguing that experiences of depression and rape "are, at least in part, products of patriarchy and are regulated by hegemonic discourses that individualize and de-politicize women's experiences."

Thus, while recognition of distress is crucial, psychiatrizing that distress can do harm, including the pathologization of relational distress and a lack of attention to socio-political (re)productions of distress such as trauma (Tseris, 2019). Such critical observations call into question the validity of psychiatric frameworks in cases of complex relational and socio-politically situated experiences. These concerns are rooted in long-standing critiques of the "failure of the DSM or the ICD to adequately represent the diversity of human experiences of distress and the role of these category systems in practices which intensify the distress of certain groups in society" (Parker et al., 1995, p. 40). Along these lines, Tseris (2019) argues that the expansion of diagnostic categories to include complex and developmental trauma risks reinforcing rather than challenging diagnostic practices and their pathologizing and stigmatizing consequences.

Such concerns are chronically and systematically absent in the mainstream psy disciplines. This absence reflects the dominance of medicalized approaches, which obscure politicized interpretations of psychological distress. Pathologization therefore acts as a key mechanism of psychiatric power and domination, setting the terms by which trauma can be understood and addressed. Here, distress is defined as an insular phenomenon with little or no connection to surrounding conditions, relationships, or power arrangements. One central problem of pathologization, then, is its individuating and isolating consequences. The figures of pathologization – the psychiatric patient; the domestic violence victim; the traumatized soldier – share something in common: they are all imagined as broken and alone. Writing on diagnosis and its discontents, Kriss offers the following dystopian reflection:

> DSM-5 describes a nightmare society in which human beings are individuated, sick, and alone. For much of the novel, what the narrator of this story is describing is its own solitude, its own inability to appreciate other people, and its own overpowering desire for death—but the real horror lies in the world that could produce such a voice.
> *(Kriss, 2013, para 15)*

Privatization of Trauma: Internalization & Marketization

Through the practices of psychiatrization and pathologization, I argue that trauma is privatized in two main ways (Thompson, 2021). Privatization in the first sense refers to psychological internalization, which is accomplished through the administration of individualized solutions to complex social problems (Thompson, 2021). Here, interventions encourage individuals to embark on a process of acceptance, focusing on individual private 'healing' rather than social, political, or relational transformation. This process typically unfolds in private sessions with mental health professionals, individual education, and/or engagement with 'expert' information (Thompson, 2021). This form of privatization is reflected in mainstream trauma-informed support services and approaches, which provide private individualized solutions aligned with medicalized and psychiatric frameworks, such as bodily and psychotherapeutic interventions. Such approaches "implicitly locate the problem within the person" (Kaye, 1999, p. 24), encouraging a process of "interiorization." Here, the individual is expected to seek out and engage with expert guidance, then privately 'do the work' to internalize and practice what they have learned.

Privatization in the second sense refers to market privatization. This form of privatization involves industries that benefit from the psychiatrization and pathologization of trauma in research, clinical practice, and the broader capitalist marketplace. In the United States, the privatization of trauma has been institutionalized through the "corporatization of medicine and the bureaucratic management of health care," and the "re-medicalization" of psychiatry (Marecek & Gavey, 2013, p. 4). Beyond the United States, this mode of privatization has been extended through neo-colonial expansions of the global mental health industry (Mills, 2017). In the process, psychiatric paradigms have joined with market interests to promote and naturalize private solutions to psychological distress, obscuring critiques of capitalism and dominant biomedical therapeutic practices (Tseris, 2019). An industry of research has supported this expansion. In the case of trauma, this has been most notable in allocations of funding within marketized educational and medical systems. Throughout the 20th and 21st centuries, funders have prioritized research examining the individual-level components and consequences of trauma in line with the most dominant interpretative frameworks, and with a specific focus on pathology. Major US funders, such as the National Institute of Mental Health (NIMH), remain focused on this priority:

> The Traumatic Stress Research Program coordinates research on psychopathology related to trauma, including research on neurobiological, behavioral, cognitive, and other risk and protective factors for psychopathology after traumatic events and the development of interventions for posttraumatic psychopathology.
> *(National Institute of Mental Health, n.d.)*

This comes at the expense of other areas of inquiry, such as the social and relational dimensions of trauma and distress, and creates a self-fulfilling industry of knowledge production. Indeed, as Rose (2019) argues, "if the key funders make it a priority to seek the brain bases for psychiatric disorders, it is not surprising to find that a very significant proportion of research on psychiatric disorders focuses on these neurobiological processes" (p. 12). Taking the example of the National Institute of Mental Health's (NIMH) Traumatic Stress Research Program, it should be noted – aside from issues with the term itself (see Bertolote, 2008) – that the domain of 'mental health,' which is the core remit of NIMH, incorporates many different approaches, perspectives, and paradigms. A sole focus on the neurobiological, cognitive, and behavioral components of pathology therefore substantially limits the scope of knowledge that is or can be produced about trauma. However, instead of acknowledging the partiality of this knowledge, researchers and practitioners have taken it up as evidence of the truth of trauma. Consequently, such taken-for-granted, authoritative discourses are rarely recognized as a product of the institutions that fund, publish, and espouse trauma research (Tseris, 2019).

Diagnostic Imperialism

The interrelated practices of psychiatrization, pathologization, and privatization demonstrate the power of the Euro-American psy disciplines to set the standards by which trauma can be known and known about. These standards have been exported globally to expand the reach of psychiatric diagnosis and its solutions (Mills, 2014). This expansion rests on the ideology of *diagnostic imperialism*, which promotes psychiatric classification and diagnosis as the authoritative way to understand and respond to psychological distress. Speaking of this "empire of psychiatry" (p. 7), Rose (2019) argues that diagnostic imperialism manifests in the authority of psychiatry to give or withhold diagnoses, approve treatments, and inform cultural beliefs about psychiatric distress and (ab)normality. And, due to the expansion of diagnostic imperialism, the experiences and phenomena that come under its scope are ever-increasing. Rose (2019) observes that it may now be abnormal for a person *not* to come under the purview of psychiatric diagnosis during the course of their life.

Most recently, diagnostic imperialism has expanded even further through the concept of 'underdiagnosis.' This has brought about a multilateral expansion of diagnostic imperialism wherein those who were not previously under the purview of psychiatric diagnosis are viewed as 'underserved' and 'undiagnosed,' and brought under the psychiatric gaze. This casts those who have not been diagnosed as disadvantaged and shores up the role of psychiatry in response. However, the potentials for harm that come with such expansions are rarely considered. In the case of trauma, this has been most evident in calls to expand trauma diagnoses beyond the DSM's PTSD category to include new diagnoses of developmental trauma (Tseris, 2019). Giving the example of justifications that revolve around the need for expanded developmental trauma diagnoses in indigenous populations, Tseris (2019) observes that "any new trauma diagnoses will reinforce psychiatry's bias towards labelling already marginalised groups of people as dysfunctional and in need [of] "fixing" rather than addressing structural inequalities" (p. 114). Therefore, rather than addressing such inequalities and approaching trauma as lodged in institutional violence, it is argued that such diagnostic expansions would instead perpetuate harm and serve dominant Euro-American power interests, "creating new markets for expert interventions, and re-casting the effects of violence and racism as evidence of mental illness, in order to justify further social control in the form of psychiatric assessments" (Tseris, 2019, p. 114).

This expansion of diagnostic imperialism also extends beyond the discipline of psychiatry and into the public imaginary. Most recently, for instance, diagnostic imperialism has proliferated through the practice of self-diagnosis, which has become especially visible in social media spaces. Here, members of the public have taken up the mantle of psychiatric diagnosis and integrated its logics into their understandings of distress and the self. In the case of trauma, social media has created a collective space for people to share their experiences. However, this has been coupled with a rise in social media 'experts' offering content and services that are mainly aimed at addressing trauma in individualized ways. I will discuss how this serves broader capitalist interests for the remainder of this chapter, but the overall expansion of diagnostic imperialism has bolstered dominant diagnostic frameworks through a process of self-directed interiorization. In response, psychiatric professionals have warned of the dangers of self-diagnosis, doubling down on the authority of formal diagnostic systems and redirecting individuals back to this domain.

The Euro-American Psy Disciplines and the Trauma Industry

In the case of trauma, the expansion of diagnostic imperialism is evident in a growing industry that promotes investment in psychiatric explanations of and solutions to trauma. Here, dominant catastrophic logics of trauma present imperatives to 'fix' the problem, actively recruiting individuals under the guise of (self) help:

> Trauma as a particularly understood catastrophe calls for relief and strategies of recuperation. It acts as the point of the sword that opens lines of entry, vectors for economic flows operating under the best of intentions; operating with the function of allowing certain bodies (ours) to be our best selves, the best of humans. This activity of opening economic flows is salved with our own pleasurable sentiments. Thus, while laboring to manage affect, to improve emotional states, to alleviate suffering, it is precisely our own affect that is turned to the work of globalizing capital flows.
>
> *(Stevens, 2011, p. 185)*

As Stevens (2016) observes, the notion of trauma "never only 'helps'" (p. 20). Indeed, a highly profitable therapeutic industry has been built around these logics of trauma. Within this industry, 'psychopreneurs' capitalize on the privatization of psychiatric care (Moloney, 2013). A vast marketplace of mental health apps offers self-help utilizing individualized therapeutic techniques. Here, users are trained to tolerate trauma and become resilient (Abdelrahman, 2023). Companies sell yoga apps offering total transformation: For a fee, women can transform their lives, release trauma, and lose weight in the process. While these "strategies of recuperation" (Stevens, 2011, p. 185) may appear and intend to be helpful (and may *be* helpful for many), they also perform the function of producing the need for urgent solutions and then providing these solutions for profit. In other words, "the therapy industry, like any other, creates as well as serves a need" (Burr & Butt, 2000, p. 186). Thus, dominant catastrophic notions of trauma accomplish the broader outcomes of sustaining the trauma industry, obscuring collective, cultural, and political interpretations of distress, and aligning the psy disciplines with global circuits of power:

> information technologies, diagnostic practices, and biotechnological expertise designed to manage bodies and to territorialize notions of embodiment, follow these flows; and with them also flow the instruments of their management: archives, inventories, tables, outcome measures, and so on.
> *(Stevens, 2011, p. 185)*

The figure of the individual psychological subject who is required and reproduced by the trauma industry can be viewed as a joint accomplishment of psychology and neoliberalism. Indeed, this industry depends on a subject who is fully invested in and committed to personal self-improvement and becoming their 'best self,' reflecting the central neoliberal demand for constant self-surveillance, management, and improvement (Gill & Scharff, 2011; Rose, 1999). Notions of the self-contained individual, and 'self-identity' on this basis, fundamentally underpin the notion of the 'healthy' psychological subject. As Potter (2009) observes:

> The normative modern self, in the philosophical and psychiatric literature, is unified, stable, and individuated from others while maintaining stable and healthy relationships with others. Those who do not experience themselves this way, or are not perceived by others this way, are viewed as mentally unhealthy.
> *(Potter, 2009, p. 18)*

There is also a gendered component to this, since neoliberalism much more consistently recruits women to participate in this project of self-management and transformation (Gill & Scharff, 2011). For example, using trauma to sell weight loss products resembles what Lazar (2011) refers to as 'emancipated femininity': a branding technique premised on the notion that women can (and should) liberate themselves from anything holding them back from being beautiful by purchasing certain products. This is based on the fundamental claim that it is a woman's right to be beautiful. In the case of 'trauma releasing' weight loss, the message is that by purchasing these services, trauma can be purged, women can be liberated, and the 'best self' can be realized.

Because notions of the self are constructed differently in different times and places, and "culture can have an impact on how the self is construed on a neural level" (Heatherton, 2011, p. 6), this version of the 'best self' – construed under the conditions of capitalism and neoliberalism – profoundly impacts how people can understand and respond to their own experiences. For instance, the autonomous, productive, emancipated, agentic, entrepreneurial, *able* version of the self that is valued within Euro-American individualism, and the version of the 'best self' instilled through psychotherapeutic practices, are one and the same:

> They [psychotherapeutic techniques] are themselves predominantly distributed to individuals through free choice in a market of expertise, rather than imposed by legal or religious obligation. They are characteristically sought when individuals feel unable to bear the obligations of selfhood, or when they are anguished by them. And the rationale of psychotherapies – and this applies equally to contemporary psychiatry – is to restore to individuals the capacity to function as autonomous beings in the contractual society of the self. Selves unable to operate the imperative of choice are to be restored through therapy to the status of a choosing individual.
> *(Rose, 1999, p. 231)*

Recently, this neoliberal push has manifested in *self-regulation* and *emotion regulation* trends and their accompanying discourses, which are steeped in the rhetoric of the choosing individual. Harvard Medical School, in its public facing materials, defines self-regulation as "the act of controlling your behaviors, thoughts, emotions, choices, and impulses… In essence, it's a type of self-control or emotion regulation." (Catanese, 2024, np). These materials explain the positive benefits of self-regulation, including the power to "keep negative emotions in check and think before you react" (Catanese, 2024, np). Rather than being viewed as legitimate indicators of discomfort or distress, negative emotions or feelings are viewed as a disruption to an otherwise happy and stable life that should be intentionally avoided or eliminated. Such negative emotions are viewed as particularly disruptive to a person's happiness, productivity, and relationships. It is argued on this basis that "while you can't always avoid negative feelings, you can change the way you react to them" (Catanese, 2024, np). Along these lines, it is implied that the best-case or ideal scenario is avoidance: choose to never encounter a negative feeling at all. This sets up an impossible ideal to which the reader is expected to aspire, nonetheless. And, with absolutely no mention of any form of culturally or institutionally bound adversity or oppression, such as poverty, the individual is expected to take responsibility for developing skills to better manage such emotions. According to these materials, self-regulation involves "emotional stability," "self-discipline," "flexibility in adapting to different situations," "persistence in getting through tough times," and "strong personal values that guide your reactions and decisions" (Catanese, 2024, np). The neoliberal imperative fully reveals itself in the concluding statement:

> People with good self-regulation skills can still feel sad, angry, or stressed during difficult times. But they have learned to manage these challenges better.
>
> *(Catanese, 2024, np)*

In contrast, those who do not master this skill are positioned as deficient in relation to those with "good self-regulation skills" and said to be prone to stress, anxiety, and 'poor' physical and mental health (Catanese, 2024, np). The contrast here of 'good' vs. 'poor' situates the individual who can self-manage as 'good' and morally superior. And, in keeping with the logics of responsibilization, those who do not succeed in the goal of self-regulation are positioned as failed neoliberal subjects who are responsible for their own demise. These logics of responsibility also serve the powerful purpose of opening realms of blame: if the individual has the power to avoid failure, they are to blame when they fail. However, this ignores one major "fiction" of neoliberal thought (Rose, 2019, p. 65); that the individual alone holds the power to succeed.

The trauma industry creates a world where trauma is viewed as a set of behavioral symptoms, interpreted as a private injury or illness, and then 'treated' accordingly. The sick individual is squarely responsible for overcoming this, but they must do so within the confines of the system that both creates and defines their experience. If they don't, they are viewed as failing, broken, and responsible for their own demise.

The mainstream psy disciplines uphold this version of the world, especially through an industry of therapeutic interventions and research that benefit from the psychiatrization, pathologization, and privatization of trauma. In doing so, the trauma industry, along with the mainstream psy disciplines, supports and sustains a broad economy of trauma that I call *trauma capitalism*: a set of socio-political and economic arrangements that leverage trauma in the interests of capitalism.

Trauma Capitalism

Trauma capitalism refers to a set of socio-political and economic arrangements that leverage trauma in the interests of capitalism, and the exploitation and commercialization of trauma and suffering for profit within global economic arrangements. This can manifest in various ways, including the creation of for-profit products or services that promise relief from trauma, and even the use of trauma in marketing strategies. Trauma capitalism relies on the commodification of trauma, which transforms trauma and suffering into commodities that can be bought and sold. This can include self-help books, for-profit psychotherapeutic services, pharmaceuticals, trauma-informed training companies, and the narratives of trauma survivors in advertisements for these products. TraumaTok and the broader raft of trauma-related content that now proliferates on social media offers self-tests, advice, and even memes, expanding the reach of diagnostic imperialism and feeding companies owned by some of the world's richest and most powerful men. We also see the commodification of trauma in popular media outlets such as films, television, and fiction books, where trauma is often used as a central plot device to entice viewers. This is underpinned by a logic of *pain for sale*, which converts the suffering of trauma into a sellable product. Again – as Stevens (2016) observes – the notion of trauma "never only 'helps'" (p. 20).

One of the most pernicious tactics of trauma capitalism is that it sells solutions on the grounds of liberation and social justice. Indeed, those working from dominant perspectives often claim to be guided by social justice goals while actively upholding the status quo. For example, best-selling books and campaigns promote science as the route to addressing trauma in the pursuit of social justice without critically interrogating the discipline of science, its limitations in the realms of trauma, and the inequities it has perpetuated (see Tseris, 2019, for a comprehensive critique). Very rarely are the claims and assumptions of science questioned, particularly in relation to psychological distress. The DSM and its diagnostic capacities are also often used to support such arguments. For example, diagnostic statistics of PTSD are often wielded as evidence for an urgent need to address trauma, often as a social justice issue, without critical consideration of the harms of diagnosis or the DSM's limitations (e.g., Bonanno, 2021; Burstow, 2005; Haaken, 2021). As such, trauma capitalism boosts elements of the status quo that critical psychologists have been resisting for decades precisely because they reflect and preserve violent social arrangements that *obstruct* social justice goals.

Another closely related tactic of trauma capitalism is its exploitation of vulnerability. This exploitation can include the use of shame to encourage engagement. For instance, as we have seen, the trauma industry offers solutions such as 'trauma releasing' weight loss, which exploits body shame (and the neoliberal imperative to do something about it) to sell products. This use of shame is intimately connected to the idealized (and fictional) notion of the choosing individual who is responsible for accomplishing their 'best self.' If they don't pursue this task, they are viewed as failing and broken. This blame and shame tactic draws on broader neoliberal health discourse, where 'good' citizens are viewed as those who take individual responsibility to manage their health, and unhealthy individuals are blamed for failing to do so (Day et al., 2020; Gillborn et al., 2022).

Trauma capitalism's exploitation of vulnerability is also evident in promises of healing and the promotion of products or services that claim to provide relief and freedom from suffering. For instance, therapy apps exploit vulnerability through the constructions of misery they purport to fix. These services and solutions exploit vulnerability by promising a 'cure.' Ironically, though, this strategic move actually works to the contrary: rather than providing a cure or addressing broader institutionalized forms of violence that give rise to trauma, these services turn trauma into a source of profit, meaning that any serious or meaningful cure would render them obsolete. In essence, trauma capitalism *requires* trauma to subsist.

Implications: Cultures of Resilience, Silence, and Recovery

As I have discussed throughout this chapter, the goal of the trauma industry is ostensibly to provide solutions to the 'effects' of trauma and offer pathways out of suffering. However, and in line with *critical trauma theory* (Stevens, 2011, 2016), I have also discussed how this constitutes and supports what I have called *trauma capitalism*, which requires and even thrives on trauma. In the final section of this chapter, I will consider the consequences of trauma capitalism and its logics. Specifically, I will consider how trauma capitalism cultivates cultures of resilience, silence, and recovery, and – in doing so – binds trauma to institutional power.

Resilience Culture

One powerful consequence of trauma capitalism is its creation of a marketized culture of resilience. Indeed, the notion of resilience is closely associated with trauma in popular cultural discourses, and "has become a protagonist in recent visions, programs, and policy interventions designed by global economic institutions" (Bracke, 2016, p. 52). Resilience in the psychological sense refers to the capacity of an individual to cope with and recover from adversity. This individualistic psychological definition borrows from the natural and physical sciences, where resilience is defined as the capacity of a substance or organism to return to its original shape after being subjected to force. While psychological interpretations of resilience acknowledge that a return to one's original state (often referred to as 'baseline') is not typical, resilience serves in both cases as a signifier of inner strength. This notion of resilience is a central tenet of trauma capitalism and its trauma industry. For example, privatized therapeutic interventions typically encourage and laud resilience in the face of trauma. And, as discussed earlier in this chapter, one major goal of efforts to intervene in the 'effects' of trauma is to bring the individual to a place of resilience and wellness. Thus, resilience is presented as a major pathway out of trauma and into 'recovery.' In fact, the *trauma-resilience-recovery* pipeline has been so tightly plumbed into popular discourse and the public imaginary that it now appears to be natural and self-evident. Those who demonstrate resilience within this narrative are revered as inspirational, such that resilience has become "a desired good, or the prize that many of us have come to set our eyes on" (Bracke, 2016, p. 53). Conversely, those who do not or cannot embody resilience are viewed as deficient, weak, and vulnerable, reflecting the ableist ideals underpinning resilience culture (Runswick-Cole & Goodley, 2013).

Related to resilience, it has also been argued that "great good can come from great suffering" (Tedeschi & Calhoun, 2004, p. 1). The concept of 'posttraumatic growth' suggests that the experience of trauma can bring about improvements in a person's life that far surpass their 'pretrauma' baseline (Tedeschi & Calhoun, 2004). The authors argue that the struggle of trauma is necessary for growth, and that this growth is inherently good. The concept of posttraumatic growth is also culturally valued. For instance, as Delker et al. (2020) argue, "individuals who tell stories of becoming stronger as a result of adversity are celebrated" (p. 244).

The authors provide empirical support from a large-scale survey study (McLean et al., 2020), reporting that "trauma stories with redemptive endings are more preferable than ones with negative endings" (Delker et al., 2020, p. 244). Feminist critics have identified problems with the cultural celebration of resilience and posttraumatic growth. For instance, Robin James' critical articulation of neoliberal resilience discourse views resilience as a specific form of therapeutic 'overcoming' (James, 2015), which hinges on a central expectation to "turn damage and deficit into surplus value" (James, 2015, p. 6). This repeats long-established racist, misogynistic, and heterosexist psychiatric discourses of sadomasochism that promote the idea that subjugated individuals enjoy pain, suffering, and humiliation (Tosh, 2016; Tosh & Carson, 2016). Here, the idealized trajectories of resilience and posttraumatic growth promote a celebratory aesthetic of suffering, where suffering is transformed into strength and becomes a precursor to personal growth and improvement.

Neoliberal notions of self-improvement and self-betterment underpin the rise and success of resilience discourse (Gill & Orgad, 2018). Here, resilience becomes intimately entwined with the figure of the individual psychological subject who is required and reproduced by the trauma industry. This individualized psychological subject is imagined outside of socio-political relations. As I argued toward the beginning of this chapter, when the individual is imagined this way, they are enlisted as both the site of trauma and its management. Here, the individual is viewed as the problem that needs to be fixed. This de-politicizes their experiences and ignores institutionally bound adversities and oppressions. For this reason, feminist scholars have argued that neoliberal notions of resilience ignore and therefore normalize the damages inflicted within white supremacist patriarchy, responsibilizing afflicted individuals to manage these damages, and celebrating those who can overcome this damage (James, 2015). One particularly cruel (but non-coincidental) twist of logic here is that women, broadly defined, typically bear the brunt of these damages while at the same time being expected to manage them. On these grounds, critics argue that resilience is a profoundly problematic concept because it normalizes and legitimizes oppressive relations and forces those who are impacted to bear the consequences. When viewed this way, it becomes clear that rather than simply emerging as a by-product of suffering, resilience is a socially constructed 'technology' that provides a forceful mandate for inner strength in the face of adversity:

> resilience is a technology of will, or even functions as a command: be willing to bear more; be stronger so you can bear more. We can understand too how resilience becomes a deeply conservative

technique, one especially well suited to governance: you encourage bodies to strengthen so they will not succumb to pressure; so they can keep taking it; so they can take more of it. Resilience is the requirement to take more pressure, such that the pressure can be gradually increased… Damage becomes the means by which a body is asked to take it; or to acquire the strength to take more of it.

(Ahmed, 2017, p. 189)

One major problem with this imperative is that, either way, it supports and legitimizes the violence of patriarchal relations: those who are willing to bear more of this violence are celebrated, and those who can't bear the violence are incompetent and must work to develop resilience. Neither scenario intervenes in the problem of violence or the patriarchal relations that frame it. In fact, both scenarios aim to obscure these damages. In this sense, James (2015) argues that resilience is part of a newer brand of postfeminism under patriarchy, where women are expected to be damaged by patriarchy, but are also expected to overcome it: "women's gender performance is a two-step process: femininity is performed first as damage, second as resilience" (James, 2015, p. 82). This, James argues, "treats patriarchy as a problem for women to solve individually. Instead of changing the world (because nobody can, there is no alternative, etc.), we must change ourselves." (James, 2015, p. 82–83). Within this narrative of overcoming, "the aim isn't a cure, but the narrative process itself" (James, 2015, p. 83). Here, resilience meets the self-fulfilling goal of trauma capitalism: its goal is not to provide a cure, but rather to promise a cure and engage individuals in ongoing pursuit. As James argues, this ultimately supports existing patriarchal logics and relations:

> Post-feminist therapeutic narratives don't just recognize that women are damaged by sexism, but *require* them to be damaged. Without misogynist feminine body ideals, what would women have to overcome?
>
> *(James, 2015, p. 85)*

Thus, resilience requires damage just as trauma capitalism requires trauma. And, rather than addressing these damages, resilience culture repackages and sells them as assets. In fact, within trauma capitalism more broadly, resilience is commonly sold back to consumers as 'empowerment.' For instance, to quote the final lines of Oprah Winfrey's book *What Happened to You? Conversations on Trauma, Resilience, and Healing*, a prime example of the *trauma-resilience-recovery* pipeline, co-authored with Dr. Bruce Perry: "in all of those [traumatic] moments, you were building strength. Strength times strength times strength equals power. What happened to you can be your power" (Perry & Winfrey, 2021, p. 298).

Cultures of Silence

This brings us to the next consequence of trauma capitalism and the cultures of silence it cultivates. When news broke of Virginia Giuffre's death, her supporters lauded her publicly for her resilience. In the following tribute, posted on the social media platform Instagram, actor and model Ruby Rose Langenheim thanked Giuffre for what she endured, revering her as a 'hero' and 'tribalizing warrior':

> Virginia Giuffre. Thank you for everything you endured in your 41 years. Thank you for your resilience and courage. We did not deserve you.
> Like many other trailblazing warriors, who risked it all to bring down an unstoppable monster. You returned home, not to a hero's welcome, but to be judged and blamed and left to fend for yourself.
> *(@rubyrose, 2025, np)*

This tribute to resilience, however, was not a celebration. It was a direct reckoning with the politics and problematics of resilience: Resilience is a very lonely place. Trauma capitalism's notions of individualism, inner strength, pathology, and privatization cast trauma as a problem to be dealt with alone, often leaving individuals to 'fend for themselves.' Within these conditions, the fundamental claim of individualism first sets up a landscape in which the person is "individuated, sick, and alone" (Kriss, 2013, para 16). Then, on these terms, they are encouraged to find support, alone. This is promoted by broader cultural discourses and institutions, leading many individuals to arrive at the conclusion that they must indeed be alone. This conclusion may be reached by an individual who is told or threatened not to tell anybody about their experience of violence, or an individual who notices that nobody they know is talking about violence. It could be reached by an individual who eventually confides in a trusted professional and is referred to discuss the matter privately with a therapist. It could be reached by an individual who, when discussing their experience with a therapist, is told to focus on reframing their own thoughts and emotions because public disclosure is risky, unsafe, or inappropriate. It could also be reached by an individual who experiences any number of these examples (and they are endless) and concludes that, because nobody else is talking about what they have experienced, they must be the only one. This cultural framing of distress is so powerful that public mental health campaigns have been developed to tell individuals that they are not alone. The true irony here is that trauma capitalism, aided by the psy disciplines, imagines and positions the individual as very much alone, no matter how inconsistent this is with the cultural prevalence of their experience. Thus, there is silence in resilience.

This is how trauma capitalism creates and operates a politics and culture of institutional silence, where silence is cast as the 'preferred orientation' (Ahmed, 2021), and public expressions of trauma are viewed as extraordinary. The phenomenon of 'speaking out' is a good example of this: When trauma is primarily understood and theorized as a private and individual phenomenon, it is expected that this will be addressed in the private sphere. As such, whether they are met with celebrations of courage or vilification and outrage, those who speak publicly about trauma are viewed as extraordinary precisely because the normative expectation is that trauma will be dealt with privately. When trauma goes public, it becomes a spectacle. For instance, the #MeToo movement laid trauma bare in spectacular fashion by uniting millions of people, many of whom felt alone, in sharing their experiences of sexual violence. With its focus on raising awareness and promoting collective action, #MeToo starkly revealed the prevailing culture of silence and rallied against it. This moment of public exposure and resistance revealed a culture of silence that is typically upheld invisibly. Indeed, feminist analyses of power have shown that established power relations typically operate invisibly, only coming into view when they are transgressed or violated:

> As we know: so much violence does not become visible or knowable or tangible. We have to fight to bring that violence to attention.
> *(Ahmed, 2017, p. 210)*

Viewed this way, the public spectacle of trauma reveals a directionality of power that would also otherwise remain invisible. For instance, 'speaking out' is often equated with 'speaking out *against*,' revealing a directionality of power. In the case of #MeToo, millions of individuals spoke out *against* the culture of silence and the institutional arrangements that protect those who do violence within this culture. As "that which must be broken" (Serisier, 2018, p. 177), silence constitutes the prevailing state of affairs within such conditions. Against prevailing power, the global reckoning of #MeToo exposed silence as "the 'other' of speaking out, as that which must be overcome through survivor speech and feminist activism" (Serisier, 2018, p. 177). In contrast, trauma capitalism – and its culture of resilience and silence – upholds these prevailing power relations and the broader cultural imperative to keep trauma private.

The fear and vilification associated with 'speaking out' also reflects the broader cultural imperative to keep trauma private. This fear is reasonable: those who 'speak out' publicly are commonly met with backlash and bullied back into silence (Alcoff, 2018). As we see in Ruby Rose's tribute, which comes from a place of support, those who go public are blamed and shamed. Virginia Giuffre and the millions who took to social media to share their stories with the hashtag #MeToo were met with backlash, vilification, and violence, of varying degrees. In the public domain, those who speak out against a problem are routinely constructed as problematic. Those who complain about violence are themselves positioned as violent; as causing damage by rupturing silence (Ahmed, 2017, 2021). This is a powerful silencing tactic. As Sara Ahmed observes, "when you do speak out, you are seen as a problem, as if the problem is only there because you speak about it. It is as if the problem would go away if you stopped talking about it" (Ahmed, 2016, para. 28).

A range of powerful institutions have sponsored this culture of silence, including the psy disciplines, medicine, and the law. For instance, like many others, Virginia Giuffre's case was settled privately out of court and away from the public sphere. Descending from the earliest insurance-based definitions of trauma, powerful institutions such as education and medicine subscribe to a legal health consumer model to manage litigation (Frazer, 2022). This medical-legal complex propagates a culture of non-disclosure and confidentiality agreements, which lock stories of trauma behind closed doors. More broadly, the fear of litigation that this creates reveals a very real fear of retaliation and backlash due to the inadequacy of legal and criminal justice responses, and the ongoing weaponization of legal systems against those who have experienced violence (e.g., Reeves et al., 2023). Those who do violence threaten and pursue libel cases against those who go public, and they often win. These outcomes are closely aligned with institutional power and privilege, reflecting "the will of the institution" (Ahmed, 2017, p. 159). Here, cultures of silence make it risky to speak out:

> There is a lot to lose, a lot, a life even. So much injustice is reproduced by silence not because people do not recognize injustice, but because they do recognize it. They also recognize the consequences of identifying injustice, which might not be consequences they can live with. It might be fear of losing your job and knowing you need that job to support those you care for; it might be concern about losing

connections that matter; concern that what you say will be taken the wrong way; concern that by saying something you would make something worse.

(Ahmed, 2017, p. 260)

In articulating the risks of speaking out, however, Ahmed also articulates the risks of remaining silent. Drawing on Audre Lorde's essay, *The Transformation of Silence into Language and Action**, she argues that "silence about violence is violence" (Ahmed, 2017, p. 260–261):

Audre Lorde once wrote, "Your silence will not protect you" (1984a, 41). But your silence could protect them. And by them I mean: those who are violent, or those who benefit in some way from silence about violence.

(Ahmed, 2017, p. 260)

Preserving silence as "that which must be broken" (Serisier, 2018, p. 177), then, serves to protect those who are violent, and not those who experience violence. This makes it more difficult to confront and resist violence. As feminist analyses have observed, "to be silenced, to not have one's speech, precludes political action" (Serisier, 2018, p. 177). These observations speak of a long history of feminist work and action addressing the politics of 'speaking out.' Audre Lorde spoke of the "war against the tyrannies of silence" (Lorde, 1984, p. 41) shared by those who experience violence, arguing that collectively overcoming such tyrannies is vital for survival. In doing so, Lorde's analysis anticipates and warns against the individualized and privatized solutions of trauma capitalism and its culture of silence. In action, 'speak-out' events during the 1970s also created spaces for resistance against this culture of silence, naming violence and promoting the collective pursuit of justice in ways that were emulated online by the Time's Up™ and #MeToo movements decades later (Delker et al., 2020; Serisier, 2018).

As with resilience, then, the culture of silence cultivated by trauma capitalism actively works against social justice goals. In response, feminist theorists have contributed politicized readings of silence, which focus on the inextricability of the personal and the political realms. This has opened up "a political opportunity in refusing to remain silent, in placing individual crisis within the larger framework of political oppression, and in resisting the cultural forms that perpetuate second-class citizenship" (Griffiths, 2018, p. 181). In her politicized reading of silence, Lorde advocates for opportunities to "speak for ourselves, instead of being defined and spoken for by others" (Lorde, 1984, p. 43). Referring to public survivor-led movements like Time's Up™ and #MeToo, Delker et al. (2020) argue that "this surge in public sharing of trauma stories is a rhetorical form of resistance to ideologies in mainstream American culture that impose silence on survivors" (p. 242). In all cases, justice resides in the battle *against* silence.

Recovery Culture

In the *trauma-resilience-recovery* pipeline, cultures of resilience and silence feed into a specific recovery culture. This defines the pathways that individuals are expected to take in pursuit of 'recovery.' Here, recovery is constructed as both a process and a destination, and it is expected that individuals will work toward the destination of recovery in appropriate ways. As I have discussed in this chapter, the goal of psychotherapeutic intervention is to get people to a place of resilience and wellness, which constructs a powerful cultural imperative for specific forms of recovery. Within this imperative, trauma capitalism defines and regulates what is to be considered 'legitimate' recovery and how this can be accomplished, based on the logics of psychiatrization, pathologization, and privatization. This may include private counseling or therapy, bodily healing, or tightly restricted litigation. Here, the same individualized logics of psychiatrization, pathologization, and privatization that underpin cultures of resilience and silence are brought to bear in the regulation of recovery:

> What better time for the ascendancy of a way of knowing injury that presents individual, whole, biologically coherent bodies as its objects of analysis; discrete and spectacular injuries that can be identified and healed, while at the same time providing technologies for managing large pools of affect and the populations understood to be defined by them.
> *(Stevens, 2011, p. 171)*

The ultimate goal under these conditions is 'healing.' For instance, in their analysis of traditional psychotherapeutic recovery narratives, Wertheimer and Casper (2016) observe that "to be traumatized meant that one was psychically wounded and vulnerable, unwhole; therapeutic practices were aimed at "restoring" normalcy or stasis" (p. 3). Whitefield-Madrano (2012) identifies four key elements of the therapeutic recovery narrative:

> 1) a once-whole, once-healthy self that was damaged by 2) a negative incident or pattern that incites a protective formula, which 3) leads to suffering–but luckily we have 4) self-awareness, the key to

returning to one's natural state of pure psychological health through a full understanding of one's "damage".
(Whitefield-Madrano, 2012)

James' critique of resilience (James, 2015) offers further critique of this therapeutic narrative, drawing comparisons with other culturally recognizable domains. Citing Whitefield-Madrano's analysis of this therapeutic narrative in the domain of body love and acceptance (Whitefield-Madrano, 2012), James observes that 'natural' health "is something that has to be *accomplished* by therapeutic labor" (p. 83). In their work examining interpretations of trauma in relation to rape, Gavey and Schmidt (2011) identified an imperative for 'healing' through such therapeutic labor:

> Linked to this imperative is the idea that healing or recovery will not be possible without the woman who has experienced rape facing it, or "dealing with it," in some way—"at some stage you are going to have to deal with it" (FG3 P2)—and going through an active process of "working through" it.
> (Gavey & Schmidt, 2011, p. 445)

The recovery imperative is expressed here in the inevitability of *having to* 'deal with it.' In this research, healing and recovery were taken to mean "getting over it" (Gavey & Schmidt, 2011, p. 445), meaning that the goal of therapeutic labor was understood as a process of getting past trauma and leaving it behind. Indeed, as the authors observe, "recovery is operationalized in ways that depict a woman being able to 'get on with her life'" (Gavey & Schmidt, 2011, p. 446). In this study, Gavey and Schmidt (2011) also found that trauma was constructed in catastrophic terms via a dominant *trauma of rape* discourse, which required specific forms of action. Here, they found that dominant individualized conceptualizations of trauma and healing informed assumptions about what should be done in response:

> The trauma of rape discourse not only sketches the nature of the presumed impact of rape, but also furnishes a set of ideas and assumptions about what should happen afterwards. As a particular instantiation of broader psy discourses, it is unsurprising that the notion of "healing" as both necessary and desirable for women who have been raped is integral to the discourse.
> (Gavey & Schmidt, 2011, p. 445)

Specifically, participant assumptions reflected dominant modes of responding to trauma as an individual problem and corresponding imperatives for recovery. Indeed, as one participant argued, "damn good counseling and support can really turn someone around, from having a terrible experience that ruins their life to putting it into a perspective where they can carry on" (Gavey & Schmidt, 2011, p. 445). In this extract, individualized and cognitivist solutions are suggested as a means to put trauma 'into a perspective' so that individuals can 'carry on.' Such assumptions function twofold to individualize trauma and the task of recovery, and define what recovery is. As we have seen, recovery is constructed as a process of individual healing, but is also "operationalized in ways that depict a woman being able to 'get on with her life'" (Gavey & Schmidt, 2011, p. 446). Thus, getting 'over' trauma and 'on with life' is constructed as the goal or destination of recovery.

One problem with individualized responses to trauma that promote notions of recovery as 'getting over it' is that the individual is again isolated as the site of intervention and transformation. In parallel with the neoliberal imperative for 'overcoming' that underscores cultures of resilience, recovery promotes the same forms of overcoming, or 'overing' (Ahmed, 2012, 2017), where recovering = *overing*. Here, recovery requires trauma to be 'over'; for people to 'get over it.' As Sara Ahmed observes in relation to racism and sexism, "there are now many strategies for declaring racism as well as sexism over… strategies that imply these histories would be over if only we would get over them" (Ahmed, 2017, p. 155). It is in this sense that 'overing' becomes what Ahmed refers to as "a moral injunction" (Ahmed, 2017, p. 155). Within the logics of this injunction, "you are asked to get over it, as if what stops it from being over is that you are not over it" (Ahmed, 2017, p. 155). Here, the individualized recovery imperative – driven by the goal of 'getting over' trauma – requires and responsibilizes individuals to 'get over it' without the same attention to the broader institutional conditions and relations that shape experiences of trauma. Here, then, the individual is located as the site of trauma and its management. This means that individuals are again constructed as the targets of intervention and transformation. As such, notions of 'getting over it' do nothing to challenge or transform the institutional conditions that allowed or cultivated 'it' in the first place. Instead, the individual is expected to move on, forget about 'it,' and get on with their life. Here, trauma is expected to be dropped from consciousness, further cultivating silence and stifling collective resistance.

Conclusion

In the first half of this book, I have considered how institutions regulate knowledge production, meaning-making, and a broad range of practices surrounding trauma. Biopsychiatric, medicalized, and individualized conceptualizations of trauma have been approached as discursive and cultural objects to show how trauma knowledge has been constituted and enacted through institutional regulation and (re)production. For example, the analysis in this chapter has revealed how dominant psychiatrizing and pathologizing approaches pit resilience against pathology and celebrate those who are able to overcome their distress. More broadly, privatized, pathologized, and individualized interpretations of trauma have been critically examined in terms of how they are informed by – and inform – dominant interpretations of trauma, inviting specific forms of action along these lines. Through this analysis, I have shown how dominant conceptualizations and interpretations of trauma inform *prescriptive logics*, which set out specific instructions for how trauma should be understood and addressed. I have also shown that these logics have specific consequences. This analysis demonstrates the power and role of institutions in both defining and regulating trauma, while also showing how institutions remain in *negative space* around dominant conceptualizations. Indeed, as I have shown in Chapters 2 and 3, institutions function to give dominant conceptualizations of trauma their shape and meaning, administer action in response to trauma, and underscore the experience of trauma itself, all while remaining out of focus. As I argued in Chapter 1, while a substantial amount of attention has been paid to understanding trauma on an individual basis, the same attention has not been paid to the institutional conditions surrounding experiences and understandings of trauma. Therefore, an institutional orientation is especially necessary to understand the role of institutions in (re)producing the meanings, logics, and practices surrounding trauma, and their consequences. In Chapter 4, I will introduce institutions in an invitation to imagine an institutional analytic of trauma, and – in doing so – imagine trauma otherwise. On this basis, I will argue that an institutional orientation is needed in order to address trauma as an institutional phenomenon.

References

Abdelrahman, M. (2023). Trauma apps and the making of the 'smart' refugee. *EPD: Society and Space*, 41(3), 513–528. https://doi.org/10.1177/02637758231173416

Afuape, T. (2011). Power, Resistance and Liberation in Therapy with Survivors of Trauma: To Have Our Hearts Broken. Routledge.

Ahmed, S. (2012). *On Being Included: Racism and Diversity in Institutional Life.* Duke University Press.

Ahmed, S. (2016, June 12). *Speaking Out.* https://Feministkilljoys.Com/2016/06/02/Speaking-Out/.

Ahmed, S. (2017). *Living a Feminist Life*. Duke University Press.
Ahmed, S. (2021). *Complaint!* Duke University Press.
Alcoff, L. M. (2018). *Rape and Resistance*. Polity Press.
American Psychiatric Association. (2022). *Diagnostic and Statistical Manual of Mental Disorders* (5th ed., text rev.). American Psychiatric Association.
Bertolote, J. M. (2008). The roots of the concept of mental health. *World Psychiatry*, 7(2), 113–116. https://doi.org/10.1002/j.2051-5545.2008.tb00172.x
Black, A., Hodgetts, D., & King, P. (2020). Women's everyday resistance to intimate partner violence. *Feminism and Psychology*, 30(4), 529–549. https://doi.org/10.1177/0959353520930598
Bonanno, G. A. (2021). *The End of Trauma: How the New Science of Resilience is Changing how we Think About PTSD*. Basic Books.
Bracke, S. (2016). Bouncing Back: Vulnerability and Resistance in Times of Resilience. In J. Butler, Z. Gambetti, & L. Sabsay (Eds.), *Vulnerability in Resistance* (pp. 52–75). Duke University Press.
Burr, V., & Butt, T. (2000). Psychological Distress and Postmodern Thought. In D. Fee (Ed.), *Pathology and the Postmodern: Mental Illness as Discourse and Experience* (pp. 186–206). Sage Publications.
Burstow, B. (2005). A critique of posttraumatic stress disorder and the DSM. *Journal of Humanistic Psychology*, 45(4), 429–445. https://doi.org/10.1177/0022167805280265
Catanese, L. (2024, August 8). *Self-regulation for Adults: Strategies for Getting a Handle on Emotions and Behavior*. Harvard Health Publishing. https://www.health.harvard.edu/mind-and-mood/self-regulation-for-adults-strategies-for-getting-a-handle-on-emotions-and-behavior
Day, K., Rickett, B., & Woolhouse, M. (2020). *Critical Social Psychology of Social Class*. Palgrave Macmillan.
Delker, B. C., Salton, R., & McLean, K. C. (2020). Giving voice to silence: Empowerment and disempowerment in the developmental shift from trauma 'victim' to 'survivor-advocate'. *Journal of Trauma and Dissociation*, 21(2), 242–263. https://doi.org/10.1080/15299732.2019.1678212
Frazer, E. (2022, February 25). *Senior Scholars, Power, and Solidarity* [Conference Presentation]. Silence Will Not Protect Us: Sexual Violence and Institutional Power in Academia, University of Oxford, United Kingdom. https://www.transformingsilence.org/
Gavey, N., & Schmidt, J. (2011). "Trauma of rape" discourse: A double-edged template for everyday understandings of the impact of rape? *Violence Against Women*, 17(4), 433–456 https://doi.org/10.1177/1077801211404194
Gill, R., & Orgad, S. (2018). The amazing bounce-backable woman: Resilience and the psychological turn in neoliberalism. *Sociological Research Online*, 23(2), 477–495. https://doi.org/10.1177/1360780418769673
Gill, R., & Scharff, C. (2011). Introduction. In R. Gill & C. Scharff (Eds.), *New Femininities: Postfeminism, Neoliberalism and Subjectivity* (pp. 1–17). Palgrave Macmillan.
Gillborn, S., Rickett, B., & Woolhouse, M. (2022). A feminist relational discourse analysis of mothers' voiced accounts of the "duty to protect" children from fatness and fatphobia. *Feminism and Psychology*, 32(2), 224–245. https://doi.org/10.1177/09593535221074802

Gone, J. P. (2023). Indigenous historical trauma: Alter-native explanations for mental health inequities. *Daedalus, 152*(4), 130–150. https://doi.org/10.1162/daed_a_02035

Griffiths, J. (2018). Feminist Interventions in Trauma Studies. In J. R. Kurtz (Ed.), *Trauma and Literature* (pp. 181–195). Cambridge University Press.

Haaken, J. (2021). *Psychiatry, Politics, and PTSD: Breaking Down*. Routledge.

Heatherton, T. F. (2011). Neuroscience of self and self-regulation. *Annual Review of Psychology, 62*, 363–390. https://doi.org/10.1146/annurev.psych.121208.131616

James, R. (2015). *Resilience & Melancholy: Pop Music, Feminism, Neoliberalism*. Zero Books.

Kaye, J. (1999). Toward a Non-Regulative Praxis. In I. Parker (Ed.), *Deconstructing Psychotherapy* (pp. 19–38). Sage Publications Ltd.

Kriss, S. (2013, October 18). *Book of Lamentations*. The New Inquiry. https://thenewinquiry.com/book-of-lamentations/

Lazar, M. M. (2011). The Right to Be Beautiful: Postfeminist Identity and Consumer Beauty Advertising. In R. Gill & C. Scharff (Eds.), *New Femininities: Postfeminism, Neoliberalism and Subjectivity* (pp. 37–51). Palgrave Macmillan.

Lorde, A. (1984). *Sister Outsider: Essays and Speeches*. Crossing Press.

Marecek, J., & Gavey, N. (2013). DSM-5 and beyond: A critical feminist engagement with psychodiagnosis. *Feminism and Psychology, 23*(1), 3–9. https://doi.org/10.1177/0959353512467962

McKenzie-Mohr, S., & Lafrance, M. N. (2011). Telling stories without the words: "tightrope talk" in women's accounts of coming to live well after rape or depression. *Feminism and Psychology, 21*(1), 49–73. https://doi.org/10.1177/0959353510371367

McLean, K. C., Delker, B. C., Dunlop, W. L., Salton, R., & Syed, M. (2020). Redemptive stories and those who tell them are preferred in the U.S. *Collabra: Psychology, 6*(1). https://doi.org/10.1525/collabra.369

Mills, C. (2014). *Decolonizing Global Mental Health: The Psychiatrization of the Majority World*. Routledge.

Mills, C. (2017). Global Psychiatrization and Psychic Colonization: The Coloniality of Global Mental Health. In M. Morrow & L. Malcoe (Eds.), *Critical Inquiries for Social Justice in Mental Health* (pp. 87–109). University of Toronto Press.

Moloney, P. (2013). *The Therapy Industry: The Irresistable Rise of the Talking Cure, and Why It Doesn't Work*. Pluto Press.

National Institute of Mental Health. (n.d.). *Traumatic Stress Research Program*. Retrieved April 16, 2024, from https://www.nimh.nih.gov/about/organization/dtr/traumatic-stress-research-and-dimensional-measurement-and-intervention-program

Nietfeld, E. (2025). What the most famous book about trauma gets wrong. *Mother Jones*. https://www.motherjones.com/media/2024/12/trauma-body-keeps-the-score-van-der-kolk-psychology-therapy-ptsd/

Parker, I., Georgaca, E., Harper, D., McLaughlin, T., & Stowell-Smith, M. (1995). *Deconstructing Psychopathology*. Sage Publications.

Perry, B. D., & Winfrey, O. (2021). *What Happened to You? Conversations on Trauma, Resilience, and Healing*. Flatiron Books.

Potter, N. N. (2009). *Mapping the Edges and the in-between: A Critical Analysis of Borderline Personality Disorder*. Oxford University Press.

Reeves, E., Fitz-Gibbon, K., Meyer, S., & Walklate, S. (2023). Incredible women: legal systems abuse, coercive control, and the credibility of victim-survivors. *Violence Against Women*. https://doi.org/10.1177/10778012231220370

Rose, N. (1985). *The Psychological Complex: Psychology, Politics and Society in England, 1869–1939*. Routledge & Kegan Paul.

Rose, N. (1999). *Governing the Soul: The Shaping of the Private Self* (2nd ed.). Free Association Books.

Rose, N. (2019). *Our Psychiatric Future*. Polity Press.

Rubyrose [@rubyrose]. (2025, April 26). "*Virginia Giuffre. Thank you for everything you endured in your 41 years. Thank you for your resilience and courage. We*" [Photograph]. Instagram. https://www.instagram.com/p/DI7TtlKzySc/?utm_source=ig_web_copy_link&igsh=MWRmaHhqY2dzam1saQ==

Runswick-Cole, K., & Goodley, D. (2013). Resilience: A disability studies and community psychology approach. *Social and Personality Psychology Compass*, 7(2), 67–78. https://doi.org/10.1111/spc3.12012

Serisier, T. (2018). *Speaking Out: Feminism, Rape and Narrative Politics*. Palgrave Macmillan.

Stevens, M. E. (2011). Trauma's Essential Bodies. In M. J. Casper & P. Currah (Eds.), *Corpus: An Interdisciplinary Reader on Bodies and Knowledge* (pp. 171–186). Palgrave Macmillan.

Stevens, M. E. (2016). Trauma Is as Trauma Does: The Politics of Affect in Catastrophic Times. In M. J. Casper & E. Wertheimer (Eds.), *Critical Trauma Studies: Understanding Violence, Memory, and Conflict in Everyday Life* (pp. 19–36). New York University Press.

Tedeschi, R. G., & Calhoun, L. G. (2004). Posttraumatic growth: Conceptual foundations and empirical evidence. *Psychological Inquiry*, 15(1), 1–18.

Thompson, L. (2021). Toward a feminist psychological theory of "institutional trauma." *Feminism & Psychology*, 31(1), 99–118. https://doi.org/10.1177/0959353520968374

Tosh, J. (2016). *Psychology and Gender Dysphoria: Feminist and Transgender Perspectives*. Routledge.

Tosh, J., & Carson, K. (2016). A desire to be "normal"? A discursive and intersectional analysis of "penetration disorder." *Intersectionalities: A Global Journal*, 5(3), 151–172.

Tseris, E. (2019). *Trauma, Women's Mental Health, and Social Justice: Pitfalls and Possibilities*. Routledge.

Wertheimer, E., & Casper, M. J. (2016). Within Trauma: An Introduction. In E. Wertheimer & M. J. Casper (Eds.), *Critical Trauma Studies: Understanding Violence, Conflict, and Memory in Everyday Life* (pp. 1–16). New York University Press.

Whitefield-Madrano, A. (2012, September 5). *We Shall Overcome: The Problem With the Body-Love Therapeutic Narrative*. The New Inquiry. https://thenewinquiry.com/blog/we-shall-overcome-the-problem-with-the-body-love-therapeutic-narrative/

4
INSTITUTIONS

In Chapters 2 and 3, I examined how trauma is defined and brought to bear through dominant institutional knowledges and practices, which define how trauma – and even the individual – can be understood. I have also shown how dominant individualized trauma knowledges profoundly shape responses to trauma within these conditions. Specifically, I have examined how individualism has separated trauma from socio-political conditions. In this chapter, I will argue that these dominant knowledges and practices are institutionally bound and produced, meaning that powerful institutions constitute the fundamental grounds on which trauma can be experienced, understood, and 'treated'. This will show that – rather than being separate from socio-political conditions - trauma is inseparable from them. I will also argue that this is not sufficiently accounted for in the mainstream psy disciplines. In response, I will present an expanded analytic of institutions and discuss some institutions that are centrally implicated in the (re)production of experiences and understandings of trauma. I will argue on this basis that institutions provide a valuable analytic through which to view trauma and its inextricable links with power, violence, and harm – both within and beyond the psy disciplines. On this basis, I will argue that there is a need to develop institutional interventions in response to trauma, instead of focusing primarily on the individual as the site of trauma and its management.

Institutions

As I discussed in Chapters 2 and 3, trauma has been defined and brought to bear through specific sets of dominant knowledges and practices, which define how trauma – and even the individual – can be experienced and understood. In this analysis, a range of powerful institutions are implicated in the production and reproduction of dominant knowledges

DOI: 10.4324/9781003042471-4

and practices surrounding trauma, including the psy disciplines, research funders, capitalism, medicine, education, law, and media outlets. Traditional psychological perspectives on institutions are typically not expansive enough to permit this level of focus. Instead, institutions have traditionally been imagined in realist terms, as the literal organizational contexts and environments in which trauma occurs (Thompson, 2021). Some examples include religious spaces, military bases, schools and universities, workplaces, hospitals, psychiatric units, and prisons. While these spaces do constitute institutional domains, the conflation of the institution with the literal organizational environment serves to obscure broader definitions on institutions beyond this space. Here, the 'institution' is viewed as an objective context or backdrop rather than a complex set of actively structured practices and relations that express specific power relations. This realist approach has been heavily critiqued by critical social psychologists because it isolates individuals from the very power relations that constitute their institutional positionality, experiences, and subjecthood (e.g., Gough et al., 2013).

Outside of psychology, institutional scholars conceptualize institutions more expansively. For instance, critical cultural studies scholars, sociologists, and philosophers view institutions as structural assemblies (Ahmed, 2017), including bodies of knowledge and practice (Foucault, 1967), socio-historical orders (Ahmed, 2012, 2017), and social, ideological, and discursive arrangements (Smith, 1987, 2005). Specifically, feminist and decolonial scholars have observed that institutions such as heterogender (Ahmed, 2017), 'the family' (Burman, 1994, 2008, 2017), white supremacy (Ang-Lygate, 1997), mainstream Anglo-European epistemology (Alcoff, 2007; Mills, 2007), and neo-colonialism (Segalo, 2015) all constitute powerful institutions that profoundly shape embodied identities and experiences. This expanded analytic of institutions encompasses ideologies, regimes of knowledge and power, and whole disciplines, extending conceptualizations of institutions beyond literal institutional spaces.

While it is important to understand how trauma arises in literal institutional spaces, realist approaches that locate and examine individuals within the immediate or literal environment are limited in the sense that they "allow the institution into the frame of analysis only as a container, as what contains what is described, rather than being part of a description" (Ahmed, 2012, p. 21). In other words, realist interpretations remove institutions as the objects of analysis, considering them merely as settings or 'containers' of individual experiences, and ignoring the active role that institutions play in the constitution of such experiences. For this reason, feminist psychologists have argued that it is important to integrate feminist psychological perspectives in psychological work, particularly in institutional spaces, because these perspectives move beyond realist perspectives, question realist assumptions and their limitations, and place an expanded focus on the role of institutions, ideologies, knowledge, and power in these domains (e.g. Thompson, 2023).

Beginning with the observation that institutions can be understood as social, ideological, and discursive arrangements, Smith (1987) defines institutions as "a complex of relations forming part of the ruling apparatus, organized around a distinctive function–education, health care, law, and the like" (p. 160). In this expansive definition, Smith argues that institutions function to coordinate local action in alignment with broad, dominant ideologies. With this expanded definition, Smith explicitly moves beyond realist definitions of the institution as "a determinate form of social organization," and instead focuses on the role of institutions as complex coordinators of social orders, relations, and practices across "diverse sites" (Smith, 1987, p. 160). As part of the "ruling apparatus" (Smith, 1987, p. 160), institutions do not simply hold social orders, relations, and practices in a political vacuum. Rather, institutions coordinate the everyday enactment of ruling power interests and organize relations among individuals, forming the conditions of everyday life. Within these complex arrangements, powerful dominant discourses propagate knowledges and assumptions that serve to organize everyday relations in the interests of established power. *Discourse* refers to the social constructions of reality and systems of meaning that are made available in specific social and historical times and places, that allow people to understand themselves and others within specific sets of socio-political relations and conditions (Potter, 1996). Within these relations and conditions, particular discourses are privileged above others through circulation by powerful institutions such as government, education, law, medicine, and, more recently, media institutions (Foucault, 1977). These dominant institutional discourses thereby come to constitute understandings of the self, others, everyday life, and social practices and phenomena; manifesting as "oppression invading our most intimate relationships, the immediate particularities of our lives, and power relations between persons" (Smith, 1987, p. 211). For instance, as Smith observes:

> We have seen that intimate and personal experiences of oppression are anchored in and sustained by a patriarchal organization of ruling.
> *(Smith, 1987, p. 211)*

It is in this sense that Smith argues "the personal *is* the political" (1987, p. 211). As such, institutions constitute and represent the 'relations of ruling' (Smith, 1987) that shape everyday life. This is accomplished almost invisibly, through the active repetition of particular ruling logics, which – when repeated – become 'institutional realities' (Ahmed, 2012). Indeed, "a reality is given by becoming background, as that which is taken for granted" (Ahmed, 2012, p. 21). When Smith (1987) conceptualized *the everyday world as problematic*, she was identifying these everyday 'realities' as harbingers of ruling relations. Feminist psychologists have argued on this basis that research must more adequately capture the interplay between the 'personal' and 'political' dimensions of experience, with an understanding that these are inextricable and powerful in terms of their impacts on understandings of the self and others, and socio-politically situated phenomena, experiences, and outcomes (Thompson et al., 2018).

In asking "what counts as an institution?", Ahmed (2012, p. 19) far exceeds the depth of critical inquiry that has been leveled at institutions in prior psychological work on the subject of trauma. Indeed, as I will discuss in Chapter 5, prior considerations of institutions in this domain typically reproduce realist perspectives, which treat institutions as 'containers' of experience (Ahmed, 2012) and omit the broader considerations of power that have been made here. Such de-politicized accounts of institutions and trauma fail to account for the role of ruling relations in shaping understandings and experiences of trauma in everyday life. Therefore, in the following parts of this chapter, I will consider some examples of powerful interconnected institutions that actively regulate understandings and experiences of trauma. These examples are by no means intended to be comprehensive or exhaustive. Rather, I will focus here on examples that are especially relevant to the discussions in Chapters 2 and 3, but I do so with recognition that there are many examples beyond these, which should be the focus of expanded work applying this institutional analytic. These examples are therefore particularly relevant to the discussions of trauma included in this book, and serve as illustrative examples that could provide an analytical template for expanded work in this domain. In Chapter 5, I will then apply this institutional analytic to critically evaluate prior considerations of institutions as they relate to trauma, and propose an expanded institutional analytic of trauma in response.

The Psy Complex

As discussed in Chapters 2 and 3, the psy complex espouses a range of concepts and practices in alignment with ruling capitalist and medicalized interests, creating an apparatus for defining and responding to psychological distress accordingly. Thus, I have argued that the psy complex is heavily implicated in regulating understandings and experiences of trauma. Here, the psy complex as an institution can be understood as larger than specific psychiatric facilities or hospitals, in the sense that it organizes knowledge and assumptions about trauma, as discussed in Chapter 2. This extends to how the individual psychological subject can be understood and imagined (Rose, 1985, 1999, 2019) and includes notions of the rational, essentialized, masculinized subject within the psy disciplines (Hare-Mustin & Marecek, 1990). Within dominant medicalized and capitalist institutional arrangements, this individuated psychological subject is imagined in isolation from their surroundings, relationships, and the very institutional relations of power that constitute this version of the self. As discussed in Chapter 3, this is accomplished through practices of psychiatrization, pathologization, and privatization, which generate combined cultural imperatives for resilience, silence, and recovery. The power of this mode of understanding the individual psychological subject is evident in the fact that, even though alternative conceptions of the psychological subject exist, it is very difficult to imagine or even locate them in dominant psychotherapeutic discourse; a point I will return to in Chapter 6.

Through a global industry of research, treatments, and interventions, this psychological subject has also become lodged in global circuits of power (Mills, 2014). For this reason, Mills (2014) argues that "psychiatric subject formation" is synonymous with "colonial subject formation" (p. 51). Drawing on Rose's consideration of the expanded "psychiatrization of the human condition" (Rose, 2006, p. 474), and the pharmaceutical industry's "massive capitalization of ill health" (p. 479), Mills (2014) charts the global expansion of psychiatric diagnostic systems. Specifically, she argues that this expansion has led to "the global spread of psychiatric ways of being a person and how we all come to understand ourselves within this register" (Mills, 2014, p. 51). This global expansion constitutes a psychiatric colonization of experience, the mind, and the self. Viewing the psy complex this way reveals how everyday practices of psychiatric diagnosis, and the definitions that enable this, are embroiled in colonial power. This demonstrates the extent of the psy complex as a feature – and expression – of ruling relations.

Critical scholars have argued that dominant conceptualizations of trauma now form a key expression of these ruling relations, specifically observing that dominant catastrophic notions of trauma from the psy disciplines serve the ruling relations of imperialism and neoliberalism:

> Catastrophe, and the "trauma" we imagine it to convey, that is, the sense we make of the injury and suffering inherent to catastrophe's upheavals, is quite central to forms of imperialism and global

neoliberalism that seem to be coming so fully into their own over the past decade. That is, what sentimentalism was to the imperial and colonial projects of the last century, where laboring subjects were brought into modernist economies as to-be-subjectified, to-be-disciplined, citizen-subjects–what sentimentality provided this great shift, trauma now provides the control society.

(Stevens, 2011, p. 185)

Speaking here in 2011, Stevens anticipates elements of trauma capitalism that have since flourished. As discussed in Chapter 3, trauma capitalism requires damage and trauma in order to enlist 'laboring subjects' in the ongoing pursuit of a cure. 'Good' citizen-subjects are those who take up this mode of necliberal selfhood and take individual responsibility to manage trauma privately. This mode of self-regulation forms a central apparatus of what Stevens describes here as the 'control society'; a Deleuzian concept referring to the shift from disciplinary power in contained institutional "spaces of enclosure" (Deleuze, 1992, p. 3), such as prisons, schools, and factories, to dispersed forms of (self) control, surveillance, and regulation. Under such conditions, the psy complex becomes a powerful institution that is centrally implicated in defining trauma and prescribing 'appropriate' responses that individuals are then encouraged to take up. As I will discuss in Chapters 5 and 6, this substantially constrains the possibilities for understanding and addressing trauma.

(Neo)Coloniality

One major expression of ruling relations is the political, cultural, and intellectual constraint of knowledge and imagination (Liebert, 2019). As I have just discussed, the dominant psy disciplines function to constrain knowledge through the colonization of experience, the mind, and the self. This implicates coloniality as another powerful institution that is centrally involved in the (re)production of understandings and experiences of trauma. In *Discourse on Colonialism*, Césaire (1972) considers colonization as an act of conquest which, justified by contempt for the 'Other', uses force, brutality, cruelty, and conflict to eliminate the 'Other' and superimpose the standards, values, ideologies, and practices of European civilizations. For those who are colonized, Fanon (1967) argues, this imposes the inescapable condition of "being through others" (p. 109). This observation grounds Fanon's fundamental argument that "White civilization and European culture have forced an existential deviation on the Negro" (Fanon, 1967, p. 14). Domination, then, is the central force of coloniality. When viewed this way, domination can be understood as a practice imposed by and on nations, knowledge(s), and individuals.

The many components of the psy complex, and those who work within these bounds, have advanced the (neo)colonial project of Euro-American political, cultural, and intellectual domination (Bhatia et al., 2023). Indeed, as discussed in Chapter 3, and in the current chapter, the psy disciplines operate as a global enterprise to export the theories, standards, frameworks, and conventions of Euro-American psychology (Mills, 2014). In their critical appraisal of the history of psychology, Bhatia et al. (2023) construe coloniality as "a system of thought, a mentality, and a power structure" (p. 63). This, the authors argue, is accomplished in the psy disciplines through "the coloniality of being and the coloniality of knowledge" (p. 62), which enforces "grossly uneven flows of power" (p. 81). Here, Euro-American-centric theories, standards, frameworks, and conventions, forged through colonial power, are treated as universal standards for humanity rather than culturally specific norms and conventions that are actively promoted over others (Bhatia et al., 2023). Some examples discussed by Bhatia et al. (2023) include culturally specific assumptions about individuality, positivism, empirical research designs, universality, history, and science itself. In charting the consequences of this colonial domination, the authors draw on Kurt Danziger's observation that psychological science was constructed on a "narrow social basis. That entailed a very considerable narrowing of epistemic access to the variety of psychological realities" (Danziger, 1990, p. 197). These constraints on epistemic access enable the colonization of experience and phenomena by theory and thus 'Knowing' observed by Rachel Liebert (2019), as discussed in Chapter 1. Indeed, "to Know was and is to capture, own, control – whether ideas, plants, peoples, or lands" (Liebert, 2019, p. 78). This narrowing has been actively accomplished through a long-standing tradition of epistemic erasure enacted through the dominant psy disciplines, which shuts down a range of possible ways of imagining psychological selves and phenomena:

> it was people's capacities as healers, sorcerers, and performers of incantations and divinations that were persecuted during the witch-hunts; capacities that enacted the liveliness of the land, the non-linearity of time, and the relationality of our selves. In order to dominate it, capitalism required that the world be disenchanted and the abilities of the body to tune into this vitality – capacities embraced by witches – be exorcised. Alienated, this new Cartesian body was

treated as a machine, as brute matter disconnected from knowing, wanting, feeling. Making its operations intelligible and controllable; constructing the prototypical individual with which Psychology is built and builds.

(Liebert, 2019, p. 7)

The culturally specific assumptions of the Euro-American psy disciplines privilege dominant Euro-American interests and idealized modes of being and 'Knowing' (Liebert, 2019). In her analysis of the psy disciplines as harbingers of white supremacy and coloniality, Liebert (2019) articulates how the scientific *desire to know* constitutes an imposition of will. Citing Stengers (2012), Liebert (2019) observes that "'Science' – in the singular and with a big 'S' – emerged during colonization as, "a general conquest bent on translating everything that exists into objective, rational knowledge"" (p. 77). This epistemic conquest – which Mills (2007) describes as "classically individualist, indeed sometimes – self-parodically – to the verge of solipsism" (p. 13) – was enacted from a standpoint of *white ignorance* (Mills, 2007), obscuring the role of 'Science' and scientists in violent hierarchies of domination, and remaining "blithely indifferent to the possible cognitive consequences of class, racial, or gender situatedness (or, perhaps more accurately, taking a propertied white male standpoint as given)" (Mills, 2007, p. 13). This is precisely how the project of scientific and thereby psychological theorizing became imbued with the goals of colonization (Liebert, 2019).

In the case of trauma, Segalo (2015) argues that the concept of trauma itself is a "neo-colonial imposition" (p. 447) that functions to marginalize and silence localized understandings and responses to distress. Thus, we can observe how the institution of coloniality is served by the psy disciplines, which accomplish the kind of 'epistemic narrowing' that Danziger (1990) observes by constraining the 'psychological realities' that can be made available. This epistemic narrowing can be seen in the fact that the specific scientific reality of trauma that dominates the psy disciplines has so extensively constrained notions of trauma that "questioning the science is seen as invalidating people's trauma" (Nietfeld, 2025, para 31). In response to this epistemic narrowing, Bhatia et al. (2023) ask the following question, which I will return to in Chapter 6:

What could histories of psychology that foreground other-than-Enlightenment—that is, based on Eurocentric White male, Cartesian dualist—rationality, for example, look like? What other actors,

experiences, knowledges, feelings, and practices might become central, and how might historians need to engage in new praxes to think, write, and feel with—rather than about—their subjects?
(Bhatia et al., 2023, p. 62)

As I will discuss in Chapter 6, this question opens up fundamental opportunities to loosen the epistemic constraints imposed by dominant understandings of trauma and generate ways of imagining trauma otherwise. I will now turn my attention to two further related institutions that are centrally implicated in the (re)production of understandings and experiences of trauma: *heterogender*, and *the family*. Based on these four examples, I will then argue that institutions provide a valuable analytic through which to view trauma and its inextricable links with power, violence, and harm – both within and beyond the psy disciplines.

Heterogender

Heterogender is another institution that espouses a range of concepts and practices in alignment with ruling capitalist interests, specifically upholding the patriarchal relations that anchor intimate and personal experiences of oppression (Ahmed, 2017). As an institution, heterogender organizes social, ideological, and discursive arrangements with the distinctive function of maintaining patriarchal power. And, due to the reliance of patriarchal power on white supremacy and class privilege, heterogender organizes power relations along these lines as well. In action, heterogender appears in gendered, racialized, and classed assumptions about appropriate gender relations, and gender itself. Some of the most fundamental claims about gender and sex within Euro-American cultures are premised on the construct of heterogender, such as dominant genetic models of binary sex that presume the subsequent linear development of cisgender identity and heterosexual orientation, ignoring fundamental evidence of sexual diversity that refutes such oversimplistic claims (Richardson, 2013). These models of sexual differentiation were constructed out of white supremacy. Indeed, as Spurgas (2020) observes:

> The idea encapsulated in early racist scientific narratives is that as the "races" became more evolved and civilized – moving up the "great chain of being" – masculine and feminine types became more distinct. The white European male was produced as anatomically, behaviorally, and physically distinct from the white European female; in some sense, the passive, receptive nature of the white European female became the

constitutive ground for white European male rationality and objectivity, while white femininity became produced as something in need of protection (in most cases from the figure of the Black male rapist).

(Spurgas, 2020, p. 11)

Within socio-cultural relations, then, heterogender grounds racialized discourses on gendered characteristics, roles, relationships, and practices. For instance, heterogender shapes assumptions about the dynamics of gendered relationships, harassment, and violence. Here, heterogender underpins racialized gendered discourses that construct women as passive and constrained (Lazard, 2020). Throughout global societies, heterogender serves a vast organizing and oppressive function, leading to material and relational outcomes wherein rich, white, cisgender men retain a disproportionate degree of power. Examples of this can be found in any given institutional realm, including medicine, law, psychiatry, politics, education, and, as we will see, the family. In the institution of heterogender, compulsory heterosexuality (Rich, 1980) reveals flows of power that 'direct' individuals into heterosexual subjectivity, othering and pathologizing those who leave this path (Ahmed, 2017; Lazard, 2020). As Lazard (2020) observes, Rich defines heterosexuality as "a political institution akin to, and underpinning, other institutions such as marriage, motherhood and the nuclear family, which act in the service of male dominance of women." (p. 5). For this reason, Rich (1980) argues that – as a "man-made institution" (p. 637) – heterosexuality must be "recognized and studied as a *political institution*" (p. 639).

The psy disciplines are also centrally implicated here. For instance, diagnostic frameworks, in their construction of 'normative' sexuality, have promoted Eurocentric colonial ideals of passive, docile, "delicate" (Tosh & Carson, 2016, p. 153), white femininity and (hetero)sexuality, and pathologized those who violate broader heterosexual standards (Tosh, 2016; Tosh & Carson, 2016). In their intersectional analysis of 'Penetration Disorder', Tosh and Carson (2016) discuss how the institution of heterogender informs psychiatric diagnostic criteria and practices. The authors argue that the diagnostic category of Penetration Disorder is problematic because it frames women's avoidance of or refusal to engage in penetrative penile-vaginal intercourse as a 'mental illness' (Tosh & Carson, 2016) in need of treatment. And, through the construction of women who avoid penetrative penile-vaginal intercourse as 'abnormal', the DSM enforces the standards of heterosexism (through the assumption that penetrative penile-vaginal intercourse is 'normal') and compulsory sexuality (through the assumption that if a woman does not want sex, she should be prescribed treatments to return her to sexual activity).

Tosh and Carson (2016) explain that such psychiatric standards of sexual (ab)normality are fundamentally grounded in colonial race science, revealing their epistemic and institutional specificities:

> The scientific study of sexuality developed out of analyses of Indigenous people as a part of colonial race science. This was the basis of, and stemmed from, the underlying assumption that "exotic" women and sexualities could be a threat to "white" and European women, as well as sexual (and racial) "purity" (Stoler, 1995). Examinations and analyses of the genitals of colonized people represented the initial sexual separation of 'normal' and 'abnormal' (i.e., "perverse") categorizations that developed within a context of violence, slavery, and colonial oppression.
>
> *(Tosh & Carson, 2016, p. 153)*

Thus, rather than being universal and grounded in biological 'truth,' these psychiatric criteria are grounded in the assumptions, logics, and interests of (neo)colonialism and heterogender. And, due to what the authors describe as a "pathologizing absence and lack of research that examines these diagnoses and experiences in relation to race" (Tosh & Carson, 2016, p. 153), these criteria and their underpinning assumptions go largely unquestioned. Here, psychiatric standards of normalcy reflect Eurocentric standards of 'normal' and 'natural' whiteness (Tosh & Carson, 2016). This analysis shows how the psychological subject becomes bound up in Eurocentric colonial ideals through this diagnostic category, and thus how the institution of heterogender operates via psychiatric diagnosis.

The institution of heterogender is therefore directly implicated in constructions of psychiatric phenomena and the psychological subject, which includes trauma. Indeed, it is argued that heterogender is directly implicated in understandings and experiences of trauma. Iantiffi (2021), for instance, identifies the colonial mode of heterogender as a traumatic realm in and of itself. In her critical reading of trauma, Segalo (2015) discusses how the institution of heterogender and its constitutive constructions of gender and sexuality fundamentally shape the experience of trauma. For instance, in the case of women, Segalo observes that sexual and gender-related violence is often driven by the enforcement of control and submission and premised on the "public ownership of women's sexuality" (p. 451), which are central components of normative heterosexuality (Lazard, 2020). And, as Segalo (2015) observes, "within a dominant discourse of male domination and female subordination, particular forces such as the material, ideological and institutional factors frame opposing experiences of what it means to be man or woman." (p. 450). On this basis, Segalo (2015) argues that the institution of heterogender shapes how violence is enacted, and therefore how trauma is experienced. Giving the example of military conflict, Segalo's analysis also gets to the crux of the absurdity of the de-politicized PTSD diagnostic category by illuminating the vastly different gendered experiences of those who do violence and those who experience this violence under such circumstances, but who both come under the purview of the same criteria in dominant diagnostic systems. This example illustrates the fundamental importance of nuanced and power-sensitive understandings of – and responses to – trauma.

The Family

The fourth illustrative example of powerful institutions that are centrally implicated in the (re)production of understandings and experiences of trauma is the family. The family has been conceptualized both as an 'enclosed' institutional space and as a broader cultural institution. For instance, while Deleuze (1992) imagines the family as a traditional 'space of enclosure', Fanon (1967) imagines the family as "a miniature of the nation" (p. 142). While both are true, in line with an expanded analytic of institutions I will focus on the family in the second sense; as a broad cultural institution and a representation of broader socio-political (and national) ideologies. Along these lines, Burman (1994, 2008, 2017) argues against the epistemic separation of the 'individual' from 'context' in her examination of the family as socio-historically contingent.

Feminist psychologists have critically examined 'the family' as a historically and culturally contingent institution to bring its functions into view. On this basis, feminist psychologists have questioned the institution of the family and how this is culturally imposed, arguing that "perhaps the most pervasive assumption about families is that they are necessary" (Burman, 1994, p. 67, 2017, p. 116). For Burman (1994) this is a consequence of the cultural privileging of families as "a universal and basic social unit," and "the site for cooperation and exchange of resources and services" (p. 67), which ignores other cultural arrangements. Accordingly, the institution of 'the family' performs powerful societal functions. Specifically, feminist psychological analyses have shown how the institution of the family, and the value attached to it, has led to a detrimental cultural imperative to preserve and protect the family. For instance, Warner (2009, p. 38) argues that "sentimental beliefs, fantasies and fictions" about the sanctity and safety of family obstruct the reporting and cultural acknowledgment of familial and child abuse.

Within these conditions, representations cast abusers as 'Other' to the ideal nuclear family, and "social anxiety is directed towards others, outside the westernized family" (Warner, 2009, p. 39). This reinforces the myth that abuse does not happen within families. One exception is sensationalist racialized coverage of honor violence, which functions to mark out and exaggerate specific ethnically categorized groups as problematic (Baianstovu & Strid, 2024). This shows how familial violence has been made visible, but typically only in service to problematic agendas.

The family is also a conduit for heterogender, which brings specific values, assumptions, and ideals about gendered and sexual relations, and organizes relationships on this basis. Because dominant institutional discourses constitute understandings of the self, others, everyday life, and social practices and phenomena, and manifest as "oppression invading our most intimate relationships, the immediate particularities of our lives, and power relations between persons" (Smith, 1987, p. 211), this includes divisions of labor, performances of (hetero)gendered roles and ideals, and violence. Indeed, as Burman (1994) argues, while the model of the nuclear family is increasingly being recognized as a fiction, "the nuclear family still continues to lie at the centre of social policy in terms of defining relationships and responsibilities (with women rendered economically dependent on men, and men emotionally and physically serviced by women)" (p. 68).

Here, heterogender functions to coordinate meanings and relations in alignment with broad, dominant ideologies, revealing again how institutions constitute "a complex of relations forming part of the ruling apparatus" (Smith, 1987, p. 160). As such, Burman (1994) observes, these discourses around the family "legitimise the maintenance of traditional gender and age roles" (p. 67). For instance, heteronormative constructions of 'the family' are interlaced with gendered and sexual discourses that specifically construct women as subordinate to men and place an imperative on women to stay with their partner no matter what, including in the face of violence. Heteronormative constructions of 'the family' have also functioned to regulate women's participation in paid work and therefore constrained economic agency. The accomplishment and performance of roles congruent with heterogender is also viewed as a positive outcome and successful sign of recovery from childhood sexual violence, meaning that heterogender is regarded as the 'correct' developmental outcome for those who have experienced child abuse (O'Dell, 1997). This promotes the implicit assumption that "heterosexuality is natural, normal and inevitable," and "feeds into the notion of any sexualities other than heterosexuality as a disruption in this natural and normal process" (O'Dell, 1997, p. 337). Thus, these gendered discourses have significant material consequences. These ideas have been actively promoted within mainstream psychological work, perpetuating heterosexism and obscuring institutional constructions and functions of 'the family.'

The institution of 'the family' also underpins some of the most fundamental claims of mainstream trauma theory. For instance, claims from mainstream psychological attachment theory are commonly invoked in public discourse and scholarship about trauma, which reproduces traditional notions of the family and lodges trauma firmly in familial relations. Burman (1994) observes that as the presumed object of attachment, primary caregivers have been regulated by attachment theory in ways that uphold traditional family relations. For example, in the traditional heteronormative family, women have been expected to perform childcare, and women who work outside of the home have been chastised for neglecting and damaging their children on this basis. Indeed, John Bowlby, who developed attachment theory, argued that "separation from mothers was an inherently traumatic experience for children" (Burman, 1994, p. 79). Indeed, Bowlby presumed that "eventually attachment disturbances regarding the biological mother would lead to pathology" (Keller, 2021, p. 44). Thus, attachment theory has been actively invoked to assign mother blame and promote the relegation of women to the private domain of domestic work. As Burman (1994) observes:

> Bowlby followed and confirmed developmental theory in assuming the presence of mothers at home, an assumption that was addressed or problematised only when a woman's full-time availability or devotion to motherhood with put in question.
> *(Burman, 1994, p. 79)*

Furthermore, it is claimed that childhood trauma can interfere with an infant's attachment type, which then significantly impacts their adult relationships. This is based on the claim from John Bowlby that infant attachment shapes the human experience "from the cradle to the grave" (1979, p. 129). Some of the most acclaimed books about trauma (e.g., Herman, 1992, 2023) invoke attachment theory to argue that trauma fundamentally violates attachment bonds and can therefore be considered a key determinant of traumatic distress throughout the lifespan. However, the limitations and problems with such claims are rarely considered. For example, research has shown that the fundamental association between attachment styles and adult relationships – which forms the premise of a range of deterministic claims about trauma and relationships – is overstated (Fraley & Roisman, 2019; Fraley & Shaver,

2000). Unfortunately, this is not broadly recognized, and flawed claims about trauma, attachment, and the implications for adult relationships abound on this basis.

Beyond questions of evidence, critical and feminist psychologists have examined attachment theory as a culturally bound and specific mode of regulating children's development, rather than a universal truth about human development. Keller (2018, 2021) has documented the universalizing 'myth' of attachment theory, arguing that it is the "WEIRDest theory in the world" (Keller, 2018, p. 11414). Referring to its cultural specificity to white, educated, industrialized, rich, democratic (WEIRD) nations, Keller (2018) argues that the universalizing claims underpinning attachment theory are based on false assumptions about evolutionary adaptation and ignore cultural variability in parenting strategies, expressions of emotion, and developmental trajectories. Further, she argues, the central assumption that the significant attachment partner is an adult reflects the cultural ideals of Western middle-class families, and again implicates the mother as the primary caregiver (Keller, 2018). Thus, rather than being a reflection of universal truth, attachment theory serves established patriarchal interests via the institution of the family. And, in *The Myth of Attachment Theory: A Critical Understanding for Multicultural Societies*, Keller (2021) notes that the fundamental claims of attachment theory remain largely unquestioned, observing that "despite the enthusiastic confessions of attachment researchers that attachment theory has substantially changed across the last 50/60 years, the basic assumptions are not questioned" (p. 147).

While these concerns may seem removed from understandings of trauma, one central problem is that, because the family is traditionally imagined as a private domain and is valued for its sanctity, any dominant paradigm that locates the origins of trauma within the family without recognizing how the family operates as an institution will push trauma behind closed doors accordingly. This, then, powerfully regulates how trauma can be addressed and reproduces the privatization of trauma, which, as discussed in Chapter 3, generates cultures of silence. Thus, 'the family' operates as a key institution that is directly implicated in the (re)production of experiences and understandings of trauma within the conditions of trauma capitalism.

Institutions and Trauma

Dominant psychological conceptions of trauma tend to avoid the kinds of complexities that arise from the institutional analytic discussed here, such as power, ideology, discourse, and social relations. These concepts are often viewed as ambiguous, and are considered to be outside of the purview of psychology due to the epistemic privileging of positivist and realist perspectives (Gough et al., 2013). Subsequently, the inextricable links between trauma and complex institutional conditions have been under-theorized, and a comprehensive psychological account of institutions as they function to inform understandings and experiences of trauma is missing in mainstream psychological discourse.

In contrast, critical scholars have explicitly identified the inextricable role of institutions in everyday experiences of violence and oppression, based on a fundamental recognition that *the personal is political*. As Sara Ahmed (2017) argues:

> The personal is structural. I learned that you can be hit by a structure; you can be bruised by a structure. An individual man who is given permission: that is structure. His violence is justified as natural and inevitable: that is structure. A girl is made responsible: that is structure. A policeman who turns away because it is a domestic call: that is structure. A judge who talks about what she was wearing: that is structure. A structure is an arrangement, an order, a building; an assembly.
>
> *(Ahmed, 2017, p. 30)*

In Fanon's account of traumatized racialized subjectivity, which is accomplished through the depiction of the *traumatogenic scene* (Burman, 2016), dominant individualized accounts of trauma are ruptured by an institutional analytic. Indeed, in contrast with dominant perspectives that locate trauma in locked memories and assume the psychiatric subject has a fundamental inability to 'know' trauma, Fanon describes trauma with a stark awareness of "crushing objecthood" (Fanon, 1967, p. 109). Here, Fanon offers what Erica Burman describes as a "diagnosis of the structure of racialisation but also how this diagnoses other constitutive dynamics at play" (Burman, 2019, p. 79). These dynamics, relationally configured and steeped in racial imperialism, are both personal and political.

Feminist psychological work has also located the suffering of trauma in institutional conditions. For example, citing Alcoff (2018), Ólafsdóttir and Rúdólfsdóttir (2023) observe that "acts of sexual violence take place in a discursive context that shapes what acts are considered violent and frames the victims'/survivors' and perpetrators' experiences" (p. 127) and "sexual violence cannot be interrogated, except by exploring the gendered context of how it is addressed (or not), framed or even justified by perpetrators and society at large" (p. 127). In doing so, the authors show how trauma itself can serve as a discursive tool to legitimize and excuse violence. As illustrated in the following extract, they show how trauma is commonly given by those who do violence as a reason for their actions:

> As a way of explaining their violent acts, they circled back to past events for answers. For example, in the excerpt below, Tómas perceives his anger as resulting from trauma. His anger causes him to lose control:
>
>> ... because of my childhood and all that, which is not an excuse; I am not excusing bad behaviour. But it's the reason why I get very angry sometimes. [...] it builds up, and every now and then, it explodes. Still, I'm always about to explode. *(Tómas)*
>
> Referring to previous trauma and reflecting on himself as damaged goods helped the participant make sense of his anger. However, at the same time it made it difficult for him to accept responsibility for it. He refers to the trauma he experienced to explain that he does not know how to deal with the feelings of anger that made him lose control; thus his trauma is unresolved. As he does not have the tools needed to deal with it, the trauma becomes a part of his psyche.
>
> *(Ólafsdóttir & Rúdólfsdóttir, 2023, p. 136–137)*

On this basis, the authors show how trauma can serve the interests of violent masculinity, arguing that "the monster is masculinity out of control, and when they lose control, it is not their fault" (Ólafsdóttir & Rúdólfsdóttir, 2023, p. 138). Therefore, a broader institutional analytic of trauma strengthens understandings of related practices, such as violence.

An Institutional Analytic of Trauma

Institutions are centrally implicated in the production of knowledge, truths, social arrangements, and embodied experiences of trauma, and therefore must be accounted for as such. An expanded institutional analytic offers the opportunity to expand understandings of institutions and their role in the experience of trauma. For instance, while it is important to examine 'contained' institutions, this should not be at the expense of broader institutions that create and shape the conditions of these spaces and inform understandings and experiences of trauma itself. In this chapter, I have articulated an expanded definition of institutions to inform this broader analytic, giving four illustrative examples of powerful institutions that are implicated in the production of knowledge, truths, social arrangements, and embodied experiences of trauma: The Psy Complex, (Neo)Coloniality, Heterogender, and The Family. In doing so, I have explored the *negative space* surrounding dominant Euro-American psychiatric conceptualizations of trauma, understanding what falls out of focus as institutional. That is: while institutions are always giving understandings and experiences of trauma their shape and meaning, they remain out of focus in the dominant psy complex.

By bringing institutions into focus, an institutional analytic not only offers the opportunity to examine the role of institutions in the (re)production of trauma, but also brings institutions into focus *as* traumatic, in the sense that they constitute the experience of trauma itself. In *Living a Feminist Life* (Ahmed, 2017), Sara Ahmed argues that institutions are 'feminist pedagogy', in the sense that we learn about feminism through institutional experiences. Just as institutions can be viewed as 'feminist pedagogy' (Ahmed, 2017), institutions can be viewed as 'trauma pedagogy', in the sense that we learn about trauma through institutional experiences. To give an example, the feminist psychological research discussed in this chapter (Ólafsdóttir & Rúdólfsdóttir, 2023) shows that trauma is lodged and operates in institutionally bound relations. Feminist psychologists have also worked to illuminate the role of broader institutional dynamics in the (re)production of trauma, as in Burman's analysis of Fanon's *traumatogenic scene* (Burman, 2016, 2019).

Because of the profound role that institutions play in the (re)production of trauma, institutions should be viewed as a primary site of intervention and transformation in response to trauma. However, as discussed in Chapters 2 and 3, dominant theories of trauma typically focus on the individual as the site of trauma and its management. The current chapter has extended the argument that institutions should be viewed as a primary site of intervention and transformation in response to trauma by examining the powerful role that institutions play in the (re)production of trauma. As such, there is a clear need to develop institutional interventions in response to trauma, rather than focusing primarily on the individual as the site of trauma and its management. In Chapter 5, I will apply this expanded institutional analytic to critically evaluate prior considerations of institutions as they relate to trauma. I will then propose an expanded analytic of trauma that treats institutions – not individuals – as sites for intervention and transformation in response to trauma.

References

Ahmed, S. (2012). *On Being Included: Racism and Diversity in Institutional Life*. Duke University Press.
Ahmed, S. (2017). *Living a Feminist Life*. Duke University Press.
Alcoff, L. M. (2007). Epistemologies of Ignorance: Three Types. In S. Sullivan & N. Tuana (Eds.), *Race and Epistemologies of Ignorance* (pp. 39–58). State University of New York Press.
Alcoff, L. M. (2018). *Rape and Resistance*. Polity Press.
Ang-Lygate, M. (1997). Charting the Spaces of (un)location: On Theorizing the Diaspora. In H. S. Misra (Ed.), *Black British Feminism: A Reader* (pp. 168–186). Routledge.
Baianstovu, R., & Strid, S. (2024). Complexities facing social work: Honor-based violence as lived reality and stereotype. *Journal of Social Work*, 24(4), 552–570. https://doi.org/10.1177/14680173231225421
Bhatia, S., Long, W., Pickren, W., & Rutherford, A. (2023). Engaging with Decoloniality, Decolonization, and Histories of Psychology Otherwise. In L. Comas-Díaz, H. Y. Adames, & N. Y. Chavez-Dueñas (Eds.), *Decolonial Psychology: Toward Anticolonial Theories, Research, Training, and Practice*. (pp. 61–85). American Psychological Association.
Bowlby, J. (1979). *The Making and Breaking of Affectional Bonds*. Routledge.
Burman, E. (1994). *Deconstructing Developmental Psychology*. Routledge.
Burman, E. (2008). *Deconstructing Developmental Psychology* (2nd ed.). Routledge.
Burman, E. (2016). Fanon's lacan and the traumatogenic child: Psychoanalytic reflections on the dynamics of colonialism and racism. *Theory, Culture and Society*, 33(4), 77–101. https://doi.org/10.1177/0263276415598627
Burman, E. (2017). *Deconstructing Developmental Psychology* (3rd ed.). Routledge.
Burman, E. (2019). *Fanon, Education, Action: Child as Method*. Routledge.
Césaire, A. (1972). *Discourse on Colonialism* (J. Pinkham, Trans.). Monthly Review Press.
Danziger, K. (1990). *Constructing the Subject: Historical Origins of Psychological Research*. Cambridge University Press.
Deleuze, G. (1990). Postscript on Control Societies. *L'Autre Journal*, 1, 177–182.
Fanon, F. (1967). *Black Skin, White Masks*. Grove Press, Inc.
Foucault, M. (1967). *Madness and Civilization: A History of Insanity in the Age of Reason* (R. Howard, Trans.). Tavistock Publications.
Foucault, M. (1977). *Discipline and Punish: The Birth of the Prison* (A. M. Sheridan Smith, Trans.). Pantheon Books.
Fraley, R. C., & Roisman, G. I. (2019). The development of adult attachment styles: four lessons. *Current Opinion in Psychology*, 25, 26–30. https://doi.org/10.1016/j.copsyc.2018.02.008
Fraley, R. C., & Shaver, P. R. (2000). Adult romantic attachment: Theoretical developments, emerging controversies, and unanswered questions. *Review of General Psychology*, 4, 132–154.
Gough, B., McFadden, M., & McDonald, M. (2013). *Critical Social Psychology: An Introdcution*. Palgrave Macmillan.

Hare-Mustin, R. T., & Marecek, J. (1990). *Making a Difference: Psychology and the Construction of Gender*. Yale University Press.

Herman, J. (1992). *Trauma and Recovery: The Aftermath of Violence - From Domestic Abuse to Political Terror*. Basic Books.

Herman, J. (2023). *Truth and Repair: How Trauma Survivors Envision Justice*. Basic Books.

Iantiffi, A. (2021). *Gender Trauma: Healing Cultural, Social, and Historical Gendered Trauma*. Jessica Kingsley Publishers.

Keller, H. (2018). Universality claim of attachment theory: Children's socioemotional development across cultures. *Proceedings of the National Academy of Sciences of the United States of America*, 115(45), 11414–11419. https://doi.org/10.1073/pnas.1720325115

Keller, H. (2021). *The Myth of Attachment Theory: A Critical Understanding for Multicultural Societies*. Routledge.

Lazard, L. (2020). *Sexual Harassment, Psychology and Feminism: #MeToo, Victim Politics and Predators in Neoliberal Times*. Palgrave Macmillan.

Liebert, R. J. (2019). *Psycurity*. Routledge.

Mills, C. (2014). *Decolonizing Global Mental Health: The Psychiatrization of the Majority World*. Routledge.

Mills, C. W. (2007). White Ignorance. In S. Sullivan & N. Tuana (Eds.), *Race and Epistemologies of Ignorance* (pp. 13–38). State University of New York Press.

Nietfeld, E. (2025). *What the Most Famous Book About Trauma Gets Wrong*. Mother Jones. https://www.motherjones.com/media/2024/12/trauma-body-keeps-the-score-van-der-kolk-psychology-therapy-ptsd/

O'Dell, L. (1997). IV. Child sexual abuse and the academic construction of symptomatologies. *Feminism & Psychology*, 7(3), 334–339.

Ólafsdóttir, K., & Rúdólfsdóttir, A. G. (2023). "I am not a monster": An affective-discursive analysis of men's perspectives on their engagement in violence against women. *Feminism and Psychology*, 33(1), 126–143. https://doi.org/10.1177/09593535221105341

Potter, J. (1996). *Representing Reality: Discourse, Rhetoric and Social Construction*. SAGE Publications Ltd.

Rich, A. (1980). Compulsory heterosexuality and lesbian existence. *Signs: Journal of Women in Culture and Society*, 5(4), 631–660. https://about.jstor.org/terms

Richardson, S. S. (2013). *Sex Itself: The Search for Male and Female in the Human Genome*. The University of Chicago Press.

Rose, N. (1985). *The Psychological Complex: Psychology, Politics and Society in England, 1869–1939*. Routledge & Kegan Paul.

Rose, N. (1999). *Governing the Soul: The Shaping of the Private Self* (2nd ed.). Free Association Books.

Rose, N. (2006). Disorders without borders? The expanding scope of psychiatric practice. *BioSocieties*, 1(4), 465–484. https://doi.org/10.1017/s1745855206004078

Rose, N. (2019). *Our Psychiatric Future*. Polity Press.

Segalo, P. (2015). Trauma and gender. *Social and Personality Psychology Compass*, 9(9), 447–454. https://doi.org/10.1111/spc3.12192

Smith, D. E. (1987). *The Everyday World as Problematic: A Feminist Sociology*. Northeastern University Press.

Smith, D. E. (2005). *Institutional Ethnography: A Sociology for People*. Rowman & Littlefield Publishers, Inc.

Spurgas, A. K. (2020). *Diagnosing Desire: Biopolitics and Femininity into the Twenty-First Century*. The Ohio State University Press.

Stengers, I. (2012). Reclaiming animism. *E-Flux Journal*, 36(July), 1–10.

Stevens, M. E. (2011). Trauma's Essential Bodies. In M. J. Casper & P. Currah (Eds.), *Corpus: An Interdisciplinary Reader on Bodies and Knowledge* (pp. 171–186). Palgrave Macmillan.

Stoler, A. L. (1995). *Race and the Education of Desire: Foucault's History of Sexuality and the Colonial Order of Things*. Duke University Press.

Thompson, L. (2021). Toward a feminist psychological theory of "institutional trauma." *Feminism & Psychology*, 31(1), 99–118. https://doi.org/10.1177/0959353520968374

Thompson, L. (2023). A Feminist Psychology of Gender, Work, and Organizations. In R. Capdevila & E. L. Zurbriggen (Eds.), *The Palgrave Handbook of Power, Gender, and Psychology* (pp. 45–62). Palgrave Macmillan.

Thompson, L., Rickett, B., & Day, K. (2018). Feminist relational discourse analysis: Putting the personal in the political in feminist research. *Qualitative Research in Psychology*, 15(1), 93–115. https://doi.org/10.1080/14780887.2017.1393586

Tosh, J. (2016). *Psychology and Gender Dysphoria: Feminist and Transgender Perspectives*. Routledge.

Tosh, J., & Carson, K. (2016). A desire to be "normal"? A discursive and intersectional analysis of "penetration disorder." *Intersectionalities: A Global Journal*, 5(3), 151–172.

Warner, S. (2009). *Understanding the Effects of Child Sexual Abuse*. Routledge.

5
INSTITUTIONAL TRAUMA

In Chapter 1, I argued that trauma can be defined as institutional in at least two ways: Through its construction and position as an object of institutional knowledge (and knowledge production), and through its experiential (re)production with/in institutional power relations. I have also argued throughout this book that dominant conceptualizations of trauma primarily construct the individual psychological subject as the site of trauma and its management. Here, responses to trauma are typically leveled at individual intervention and transformation, foreclosing opportunities for institutional intervention and transformation in response to trauma. Having examined the knowledges and practices that reveal trauma as an object of institutional knowledge in Chapters 2 and 3, and introduced institutions in Chapter 4, I will now turn attention to understanding trauma in the second sense, by articulating the experiential (re)production of trauma with/in institutional power relations. Here, I will be guided by the need for institutional intervention and transformation in response to trauma, which I proposed in Chapter 4. I will begin by examining prior work on trauma and institutions, focusing on two major theories-*institutional betrayal* and *systemic trauma*-which currently dominate thinking around the role of institutions in the (re) production of trauma. Specifically, I will evaluate these theories in terms of how they conceptualize *institutions* and *trauma*. I will also consider the extent to which these theories conceptualize institutions as sites for intervention and transformation. Based on this evaluation, I will argue that these two dominant theories can be viewed as incongruent with an expanded institutional analytic of trauma because they both rely on dominant assumptions and practices derived from the psy disciplines, and both focus on the individual psychological subject as the site of trauma and its management. In response, I will propose an institutional analytic of trauma to articulate the experiential (re)production of trauma with/in institutional power relationships and conceptualize

DOI: 10.4324/9781003042471-5

trauma as a relational and situated institutional phenomenon. In doing so, I will outline a need for conceptual tools that enable institutional intervention and transformation in response to trauma, which will be the focus of Chapter 6.

Trauma and Institutions

Popular mainstream theorizing around trauma in relation to institutions largely draws on two major theories: *Institutional betrayal* and *systemic trauma*. In 2021, I argued that 'institutional betrayal' is increasingly being deployed as an explanatory theory for 'institutional trauma' (Thompson, 2021). For instance, a cursory internet search for the term 'institutional trauma,' and even the most rigorous academic literature search, reveals that these terms are considered to be virtually synonymous (Thompson, 2021). 'Systemic trauma' is a theory that invokes institutions based on the observation that systemic conditions can (re) produce trauma. Systemic trauma refers to trauma that arises from long-standing or widespread violence that is enabled on a grand scale by societal institutions. To understand how trauma has been understood in relation to institutions in prior work, I will now evaluate both theories in terms of how they conceptualize *institutions* and *trauma*. I will also consider the extent to which these theories conceptualize institutions as sites for intervention and transformation in response to trauma.

Institutional Betrayal

As I have observed, *institutional betrayal* is increasingly being deployed as an explanatory theory for 'institutional trauma.' This is by far the most dominant theoretical framework used in contemporary research exploring institutions and trauma. As such, it seems that *institutional betrayal* has achieved the status of a totalizing theory of 'institutional trauma.' Institutional betrayal typically refers to the notion of institutions doing nothing or failing individuals, particularly when they report instances of violence and distress. Drawing on *betrayal trauma* theory (Freyd, 1994), Smith and Freyd (2014) define 'institutional betrayal' as "individual experiences of violations of trust and dependency perpetrated against any member of an institution" (p. 577). In this work, the authors focus on understanding interpersonal mistreatment within institutional contexts such as schools, colleges, the military, and legal systems. In their elaboration of the concept of 'institutional betrayal,' the authors identify deficits and failures in institutional processes as key institutional mechanisms that function to (re)produce or compound trauma (Smith &

Freyd, 2014). Typically, this manifests in instances of negligence, incompetence, or betrayals of trust. However, while the notion of institutional betrayal observes that specific institutional dynamics may compound the experience of trauma, this does not equate to a comprehensive explanatory theory of 'institutional trauma,' as is commonly assumed. There are two main premises of *institutional betrayal* theory that illustrate this specificity, and are incongruent with the expanded institutional analytic of trauma discussed thus far.

Locating 'Trauma' in Institutional Betrayal

The first incongruent premise of institutional betrayal theory is its conceptualization of trauma in line with the dominant psy disciplines. More precisely, the theory of *betrayal trauma* (Freyd, 1994) that underpins the theory of *institutional betrayal* does not locate trauma in institutional relations. This is a "theory of psychogenic amnesia for childhood abuse" (Freyd, 1994, p. 309). Based on evolutionary and cognitive psychological perspectives, the original aim of this theory was to improve understandings of amnesia in instances of child sexual abuse. Here, notions of trauma are treated neither as institutionally produced nor located. Indeed, as I have previously observed:

> Couched in a language of symptomology and adaptation, this concept of trauma is aimed at understanding the specific bodily impacts of abuse, particularly on memory repression and impairment. Thus, the theoretical concept of trauma underpinning the theory of "institutional betrayal" is not concerned with the kind of socio-political analysis needed to examine institutions. This is further evidenced by the fact that there are no clear definitions, theoretical engagements, or conceptualizations of "institutions" in explanations of "institutional betrayal".
> *(Thompson, 2021, p. 111)*

This raises questions over why, in a theory of *institutional* trauma, such highly individualized and biological assumptions are the focus. Indeed, much work has been done to understand trauma based on such individualized and biological perspectives, while comparatively little attention has been paid to understanding trauma as an institutional phenomenon. Based on this, one would expect institutional theories to elaborate extensively on the institutional dimensions of this phenomenon. So, again, why conceptualize trauma otherwise? The answer to this question should at this point be somewhat evident: As discussed throughout this book, there is a vast institutional psy complex that promotes these dominant individualized and biological assumptions at the expense of others. As such, dominant conceptualizations of trauma are left intact. Instead of conceptualizing trauma as an institutional phenomenon, dominant individualized definitions of trauma are picked up and dropped into institutional contexts. Indeed, much of the research leaves dominant individualized conceptualizations of *betrayal trauma* intact through an *absence* of critical interrogation, which leaves the audience to rely on taken-for-granted meanings and assumptions about trauma, and what Stevens (2011) refers to as "a very powerful and felt sense that we know what we mean when we do" (p. 175).

For example, in a special issue of 6 articles published in *Trauma and Dissociation* with a focus on trauma and institutions (Filippaki & Salter, 2021), Smith (2021) acknowledges that trauma itself is not the focus of the work: "the interest of this article is not to make explicit the forms of trauma which these types of [institutional] disputes may produce, but instead to draw attention to how institutional forms can produce the conditions of possibility for trauma" (Smith, 2021, p. 474–475). This exemplifies the scarcity of critical interrogation afforded to 'trauma' in previous work in this domain. Here, due to an absence of critical interrogation, dominant conceptualizations of trauma are accepted at face value and trauma is cast back into the individualized psychological subject, leaving the institutional dimensions of trauma itself unexamined. On this basis, the individual is again imagined as the site of trauma and its management. As discussed in Chapters 2, 3, and 4, this perspective is problematic because it isolates individuals from the very power relations that constitute their institutional experiences, and obscures the role of institutions in the (re)production of trauma. This makes a critical institutional analytic of trauma all the more necessary and leads to the second incongruent premise of *institutional betrayal*, which lies in how the 'institutional' domain is conceptualized.

Locating the 'Institution' in Institutional Betrayal

The second premise of institutional betrayal theory that is incongruent with an expanded institutional analytic lies in its definition of the 'institution.' As discussed, Smith and Freyd (2014) define 'institutional betrayal' as "individual experiences of violations of trust and dependency perpetrated against any member of an institution" (p. 577) and focus on understanding this within institutional contexts such as schools, colleges, the military, and legal systems. As discussed in Chapter 4, this replicates traditional understandings of institutions from a realist perspective, conceptualizing institutions as the literal organizational spaces or 'containers' (Ahmed, 2012) in which interpersonal betrayals take place and trauma occurs. In conjunction with the notion of *betrayal trauma* that underpins this theory, this again casts trauma back into the individualized psychological subject.

Much of the subsequent work examining *institutional betrayal* also conceptualizes the institution as the organizational context in which trauma takes place. For instance, in the special issue of *Trauma and Dissociation* discussed earlier, Smith (2021) defines 'the institution' as the organizational context of the university. While this work provides valuable insights into the dynamics and workings of such institutions, it conceptualizes the institution narrowly as a literal organizational domain. Here, the institution serves as the context in which traumatic events happen to individuals, rather than a broad and complex assembly of socially negotiated power relations. Such narrow conceptualizations of 'the institution' as a literal organizational space typically focus on understanding how trauma might show up in such contexts. Locating trauma within this objective space constructs trauma passively as something that happens in – and not as a product or feature of – institutions. This casts trauma as 'Other' to the institution, again taking trauma at face value, while leaving the institutional dimensions of trauma unexamined.

An expanded institutional analytic has therefore been lacking in prior work on institutions and trauma; even and especially in work that refers directly to institutions. There have been calls to address this gap, but the work remains limited. To give the example of the special issue of *Trauma and Dissociation*, this collection built on the theory of institutional betrayal (Smith & Freyd, 2014), explicitly identifying a need to account for 'the institution' in relation to trauma. In this collection, Smith (2021) argued that "to understand institutional trauma, we first need to understand the institution" (p. 466). This declaration of a fundamental need to understand 'the institution' demonstrates the need for more expansive institutional accounts of trauma. Such an expansion is needed in order to avoid reproducing assumptions and perspectives that ultimately allow for institutional distancing and support established institutional power interests. Indeed, when individualized notions of trauma are left intact, the traumatized (individual) subject and their trauma can be viewed in isolation from institutions. For instance, it has been argued that it is no surprise that universities tend to promote dominant individualized psychological models in their conceptualizations of mental health and wellbeing. As Khúc (2024) argues, universities rely on this model to responsibilize individuals for managing the unwellness that arises from institutional conditions:

> Counseling centers are institutional creations, beholden to the larger institution. Counselors are trained in fields that are their own institutions — most often psychology and psychiatry — from which we inherit the medical model of mental health, of individual pathology to be cured. And all institutions are in the business of subject formation — of shaping us into beings that function within those institutions.
> … students are being crushed by a *Titanic* that tells them (and even thinks) it is helping them. And as they are being crushed, they are told they need to fix themselves — to learn better time management, to drink less, to procrastinate less, to tolerate distress better, to sleep more, and of course, to *go to the counseling center* — so that they can go back to being good, productive students again.
> *(Khúc, 2024, p. 37)*

Here, the politics of epistemic dominance are revealed in the reproduction of the dominant medical model of mental health, which is actively imposed in the space of the university through the institutional creation of counseling services and wellness centers. This reveals not only the status of the psy disciplines and (neo)colonialism as powerful institutions, but also how these broader institutions operate powerfully within specific organizational settings. This further demonstrates the need for an expanded institutional analytic that recognizes institutions as "a complex of relations forming part of the ruling apparatus, organized around a distinctive function– education, health care, law, and the like" (Smith, 1987, p. 160), rather than simply 'containers' of experience. This expanded analytic would allow for interventions to be directed at institutional transformation.

As I have noted, 'institutional betrayal' is increasingly being conflated and deployed as a totalizing theory of 'institutional trauma.' However, while this theory does identify how some institutional dynamics can play a role in the institutional (re)production of trauma, this is by no means a totalizing theory of the role that institutions can play in the (re) production of trauma, and therefore cannot be viewed as synonymous with 'institutional trauma.' While the theory of institutional betrayal cites institutions as a central concern, these are understood as 'factors' or characteristics of "settings in which traumatic events are more likely to transpire" (Smith & Freyd, 2014, p. 580), rather than the very stuff of which trauma is made. Thus, 'institutional betrayal' could be understood as one facet of 'institutional trauma,' but not as a synonymous term or totalizing theory, as is commonly assumed.

Systemic Trauma

Systemic trauma is the second major theory that invokes institutions to understand experiences of trauma. In response to highly individualized conceptualizations of trauma, researchers have drawn attention to the 'systemic' features of trauma in order to understand how broader social conditions 'give rise to' trauma. Here, the experience of trauma is viewed in the context of social systems, which are broadly defined, from schools and other 'contained' spaces through to systems of oppression, such as colonization, imperialism, and genocide (Haines, 2019).

Locating 'Trauma' in Systemic Trauma

Those who study systemic trauma focus on the effects of institutions on (post)traumatic responses, and define systemic trauma as follows:

> Systemic trauma refers to the contextual features of environments and institutions that give rise to trauma, maintain it, and impact posttraumatic responses. The systemic trauma framework is informed by ecological models that emphasize the contributions of families, schools, communities, and cultures to psychological functioning (e.g., Casey & Lindhorst, 2009; Reilly & Gravdal, 2012); feminist models that highlight external conditions that influence trauma and its effects (e.g., Herman, 1992; Hornstein, 2013); models within the social work, nursing, and global health fields that advocate social, structural, and policy changes to improve posttraumatic outcomes (Hatcher et al., 2013; Healy, 2012; Lucero & Bussey, 2012); and human rights perspectives that champion broad-based initiatives for trauma prevention and intervention (Ahn et al. 2013; Beske, 2009; Newman, 2013; Ray, 2008). A systemic trauma approach aligns with multidisciplinary efforts to reduce trauma and traumatic stress.
> *(Goldsmith et al., 2014, p. 118)*

Within this definition, the authors refer to several institutional realms, including families, schools, and communities, that 'give rise to' trauma. However, despite this focus on "the contextual features of environments and institutions" (Goldsmith et al., 2014, p. 118), this theory still centers the individual psychological subject, casting them as the site of trauma and its management. Within this interpretation, trauma is conceptualized as an outcome in its own right rather than an inherently institutional phenomenon. As with the theory of institutional betrayal, this means that dominant individualized definitions of trauma are again picked up and dropped into institutional contexts. Specifically, this definition leaves the dominant individualized *Trauma* ⇔ *PTSD* framework intact through a reliance on dominant assumptions about 'posttraumatic responses,' 'trauma and its effects,' 'posttraumatic outcomes,' and 'traumatic stress.' Coupled with an absence of critical interrogation, this again leaves the audience to rely on taken-for-granted meanings and assumptions about trauma.

In this definition, the main target of trauma intervention is to "improve posttraumatic outcomes" (Goldsmith et al. 2014, p. 118). Here, the individual psychological subject – as imagined by the dominant psy disciplines and defined through the lens of posttraumatic pathology – is the main focus of such interventions in response to trauma. This is more explicitly iterated in arguments about how to respond to systemic trauma:

> The research is clear that the consequences of trauma extend far beyond PTSD symptoms to include depression, other anxiety symptoms, substance use, physical health problems, alexithymia, dissociation, and emotion regulation difficulties (e.g., Freyd, et al. 2005; Grant, Cannistraci, Hollon, Gore, & Shelton, 2011; O'Brien & Sher, 2013; Subica, Claypoole, & Wylie, 2012). Besides failing to reflect the current state of the science, a narrow focus on PTSD may restrict research funding for and attention to research that addresses other important antecedents and outcomes of trauma and thereby limit both scientific developments and potentially helpful interventions.
> *(Goldsmith et al., 2014, p. 119)*

Through the lens of psychiatrization, pathologization, and privatization, the individuated psychological subject is invoked in this account of systemic trauma in order to justify an expanded diagnostic gaze over trauma. Here, the case is made for broader diagnostic interventions based on the *limitations* of the PTSD category. As discussed in Chapter 3, this extends the reach of diagnostic imperialism and squarely locates trauma within individuals as a pathology. Thus, the focus here is not on institutional or systemic transformation, but instead on individual intervention.

This raises larger questions over the inconsistencies between the stated definition of systemic trauma and the focus of responses. For instance, Goldsmith et al. (2014, p. 119) argue that "systemic trauma refers to the contextual features of environments and institutions that give rise to trauma, maintain it, and impact posttraumatic responses." To give another example, it has been argued that "systemic trauma is the repeated, ongoing violation, exploitation, dismissal of, and/or deprivation of groups of people" (Haines, 2019, p. 80). In both examples, systemic trauma is defined in terms of institutional conditions and dynamics. Specifically, trauma is located in the contextual features of environments, and more specifically as violence and exploitation. However, the focus of responses is on the 'effects' of this, as though this constitutes the trauma. While this serves as a prime example of trauma being used to simultaneously describe both events and their impacts, where "the trauma [event] has caused a trauma [reaction]" (Tseris, 2019a, p. 687), focusing on the reaction reveals that it is not the contextual features of environments that are treated as sites for intervention and transformation, but rather the individual.

Therefore, while the theory of systemic trauma was developed in order to account for the institutional conditions that contribute to trauma, the understanding of trauma at the center of this theory is implicitly based on dominant individualized conceptualizations from the psy disciplines that are left inherently intact. This argument can be extended by examining how the theory of systemic trauma imagines the individual in relation to institutions. Indeed, in the ecological models that inform systemic trauma theory, the individual is imagined as a discrete and self-contained entity in line with the dominant mainstream psy disciplines. As we saw in Chapters 2 and 3, this self-contained notion of the individual is so powerful that it has become privileged as the dominant way of conceptualizing the self in neoliberal cultures. This leads to broader concerns over conceptualizations of 'the individual' within systemic trauma theory.

Locating the 'Institution' in Systemic Trauma

The theory of systemic trauma is grounded in systems theory. This systems theory was developed in Austria in the 1930s as a 'major scientific movement' by Ludwig von Bertalanffy (Lilienfield, 1978, p. 16), from the concept of the 'open system.' As the historic record shows, von Bertalanffy aligned his theoretical contributions with the ideologies of Nazism, framing his systems theory as a contribution to German nationalist ideology (O'Neill, n.d.). Originating from the discipline of biology, this grew into an interdisciplinary formulation of a *general system theory*, unified by scientific laws and principles (Lilienfield, 1978). Upon emigrating to the United States via the United Kingdom and Canada in the 1950s, von Bertalanffy aligned his general system theory with the American theory of *cybernetics*. Cybernetics is largely attributed to Norbert Wiener, an American computer scientist who proposed that, just like organisms in the 'natural' world, individual humans were connected by a complex network (Wiener, 1948, 1961). On this basis, Wiener viewed human organisms as machines, processing information via a complex system of feedback loops. For instance, the brain was imagined as a computer, processing and acting on information and feedback from the world.

Borrowing from the natural sciences, systems theory was predicated on the notion of the 'ecosystem.' Here, human beings, organizations, and whole societies were imagined as components, or nodes, in complex and dynamic self-organizing ecosystems. It was argued that these ecosystems would naturally balance themselves through the principle of 'equilibrium'; a term that was also borrowed from the natural sciences. Specifically, it was argued that equilibrium, through its production of self-organization, was how human societies maintained their structure. In social scientific extrapolations of systems theory, individuals were imagined as part of this machine-like network of social organization (Lilienfield, 1978). Systems theory thus borrowed concepts and principles from the natural sciences and merged them with emerging cognitivist concepts amidst the rise of computer technologies in the 1950s.

In the disciplines of psychology and social work, and particularly in the discipline of American community psychology, von Bertalanffy's systems theory has been taken up enthusiastically to explain how the individual can be understood in a broader social context. For instance, Urie Bronfenbrenner's *Ecological Systems Theory*, which has been cited extensively in the domains of community psychology and social work, is an adaptation of von Bertalanffy's systems theory (Bowers & Bowers, 2017). Bronfenfrenner's Ecological Systems Theory, which he later updated to the *Bioecological Model*, is grounded in the positivist and experimentalist episteme of the dominant American psy disciplines. In its first articulation, *Toward an Experimental Ecology of Human Development*, Bronfenbrenner (1977) argued that individualistic theories of human development were insufficient and did not capture the dynamic relations between individuals and social contexts. Here, Bronfenbrenner advocated for "a broader approach to research in human development that focuses on the progressive accommodation, throughout the life span, between the growing human organism and the changing environments in which it actually lives and grows" (p. 513):

> While human beings have been studied in a variety of environments, there are few investigations in which the behavior and development of the *same* persons have been examined as a function of their exposure to *different* settings.
>
> *(Bronfenbrenner, 1977, p. 522)*

Bronfenbrenner conceptualized this changing relationship between the environment as "conceived in systems terms" (p. 513). His original theory identified a series of systems surrounding the individual: The *microsystem, mesosystem, exosystem, macrosystem, and chronosystem* (Bronfenbrenner, 1977). In visual representations of Bronfenbrenner's Ecological Systems Theory, these systems are depicted as a series of circular rings. The individual is typically depicted as the central point within this series of expanding circular rings. Here, the individual is in the center, with context expanding around them. This is designed to communicate the 'nested' nature of systems, where the individual is nested within these systems, which are in turn nested within each other. Here, the individual is imagined as a discrete entity around which these systems revolve.

Bronfenbrenner advocated for the use of experimental methods to ascertain the properties of systems and their effects:

> The point being made is a positive one—namely, that the experiment plays a critical role in ecological investigation not only for testing hypotheses but, at prior stages, for detecting and analyzing systems properties within the immediate setting and beyond. The special suitability of the experiment for this purpose is highlighted by an adaptation of Dearborn's dictum to the ecological realm: *If you wish to understand the relation between the developing person and some aspect of his or her environment, try to budge the one, and see what happens to the other.* Implicit in this injunction is the recognition that the relation between person and environment has the properties of a system with a momentum of its own; the only way to discover the nature of this inertia and its interdependencies is to try to disturb the existing balance.
>
> *(Bronfenbrenner, 1977, p. 518)*

In doing so, he invoked the core principles of systems theory, arguing that "the relation between person and environment has the properties of a system with a momentum of its own" (Bronfenbrenner, 1977, p. 518). Here, the concept of the system with a 'momentum of its own' – unified by scientific laws and principles, and knowable as such – is characterized by a natural inertia that can be observed via its 'existing balance' or changes thereto. The systems component of *systemic trauma* theory therefore conceptualizes the individual's experience of trauma as resulting from features or changes to the environment that the individual is exposed to, which 'gives rise to' trauma.

There are, however, some limitations with the application of systems theory as a comprehensive explanatory theory of 'institutional trauma' on this basis. These limitations arise in relation to the expanded institutional analytic developed in Chapters 2, 3, and 4, but also align with broader critiques of systems theory as applied to complex human experiences. Firstly, the location of the individual at the center of the theory not only prioritizes the notion of the self-contained individual but also views them as the epicenter of the phenomenon under construction. This self-centered neoliberal version of the self prioritizes Euro-American notions of selfhood and ignores alternative modes of understanding the self, including critical observations that the self is relational, plural, socio-politically located, and historically contingent (Gallagher, 2013; Gergen, 1971). It also reinscribes the individuated psychological subject as the site of trauma and its management. Thus, interventions remain firmly focused on the individual rather than institutions.

Another limitation of a systems theory approach, which I also discussed in relation to *institutional betrayal* theory, is that systems theory conceptualizes systems as a series of objective environments to which the individual is 'exposed.' The assumption is that the context or environment acts on the individual who can be understood experimentally as a discrete entity in isolation from that context. Objective and experimentalist conceptualizations of 'exposure' to contexts and environments have been heavily critiqued by critical psychologists who argue that social context is actively constructed and serves particular interests based on dominant power relations, thereby rendering the individual inextricable from these dynamics (e.g., Gergen, 2015; Gough et al. 2013; Potter, 1996). Due to the experimentalist tradition in the domain of systems science, ecological and systems theories largely avoid the complex social, ideological, and discursive arrangements that fundamentally inform individual experiences and subjectivities. As such, the systems theories underpinning systemic trauma theory are not congruent with an expanded analytic of institutions. Indeed, as we saw in arguments from Goldsmith et al. (2014) about how to respond to systemic trauma, individuals – not institutions – remain the focus of intervention and transformation efforts from this perspective.

Then, there is the larger question of the flawed logic of *ecosystems* underpinning systems theory, which brings this theoretical framework into question more broadly. I credit documentary filmmaker Adam Curtis with this most fundamental concern. Released in 2011, Curtis' three-part documentary series, *All Watched Over by Machines of Loving Grace*, charted the rise of the technological revolution in America, and its global political implications. In episode two, *The Use and Abuse of Vegetational Concepts* (Curtis, 2011a), Curtis critically examined the rise of systems theory at this time. In an accompanying article, Curtis

(2011b) elucidated the invention of the concept of ecosystems by botanist Arthur Tansley in the 1920s:

> It all started with a dream. One night Tansley had an unsettling nightmare that involved him shooting his wife. So he did the natural thing and started reading the works of Sigmund Freud, and even went to be analysed by Freud himself. Then Tansley came up with an extraordinary theory. He took Freud's idea that the human brain is like an electrical machine – a network around which energy flowed – and argued that the same thing was true in nature. That underneath the bewildering complexity of the natural world were interconnected systems around which energy also flowed. He coined a name for them. He called them ecosystems.
>
> But Tansley went further. He said that the world was composed at every level of systems, and what's more, all these systems had a natural desire to stabilise themselves. He grandly called it "the great universal law of equilibrium". Everything, he wrote, from the human mind to nature to even human societies – all are tending towards a natural state of equilibrium.
>
> Tansley admitted he had no real evidence for this. And what he was really doing was taking an engineering concept of systems and networks and projecting it on to the natural world, turning nature into a machine. But the idea, and the term "ecosystem", stuck.
>
> *(Curtis, 2011b, para 11–13)*

Rather than offering supportive evidence for notions of equilibrium and inertia in ecosystems, scientists ultimately repudiated such claims. Indeed, in the same article – and as documented in the second episode of *All Watched Over by Machines of Loving Grace* – Curtis (2011b) observes that in the 1960s:

> a new generation of ecologists began to question the very basis of Arthur Tansley's idea of the self-regulating ecosystem. Out of this came a bloody battle within the science of ecology, with the new generation showing powerfully that wherever they looked in nature they found not stability, but constant, dynamic change; that Tansley's idea of a underlying pattern of stability in nature was really a fantasy, not a scientific truth.
>
> *(Curtis, 2011b, para 25)*

This 'fantasy' has created far-reaching implications. For instance, it has contributed to problematic ideas of resilience, which are rooted in the assumption that ecosystems always work to maintain equilibrium. Indeed, the basic definition of resilience is the capacity of a system or organism to recover or 'bounce back' after being altered by a disturbance. As discussed in Chapter 3, this idea has been extrapolated and applied to humans in problematic ways. The revelation of this fundamental theoretical flaw therefore not only brings systems theory into question but also brings its associated concepts into question with it. In the case of resilience this adds to mounting critiques, which I discussed in Chapter 3 and will return to in Chapter 6.

Another problem is that while Bronfenbrenner critiqued the artificiality of classic experimental paradigms, he responded to this by advocating for *more* science. In doing so, he critiqued qualitative and participant-driven approaches as lacking in scientific rigor:

> one major foundation has recently stated as its new policy that, henceforth, grants for research will be awarded only to persons who are themselves the victims of social injustice. Other, less radical expressions of this trend involve reliance on existential approaches in which "experience" takes the place of observation and analysis is foregone in favor of a more personalized and direct "understanding" gained through intimate involvement in the field situation. More common, and more scientifically defensible, is an emphasis on naturalistic observation, but with the stipulation that it be unguided by any hypotheses formulated in advance and uncontaminated by structured experimental designs imposed prior to data collection.
> *(Bronfenbrenner, 1977, p. 514)*

In response, he doubled down on the value of 19th- and 20th-century scientific methods:

> In my view, 20th-century science possesses research strategies that, had they been available to the 19th-century naturalists, would have enabled them to leapfrog years of painstaking, exhaustive description in arriving at a formulation of biographical principles and laws. This is not to imply that taxonomy is not an essential scientific task but only to assert that a phase of comprehensive observation, recording, and classification may not be a necessary condition for making progress in the understanding of process, and that the early application of experimental paradigms may in fact lead to more appropriate taxonomies for achieving the requisite work of systematic description.
> *(Bronfenbrenner, 1977, p. 514)*

In doing so, he conjured the authority of the traditional scientific *desire to know* that has been heavily critiqued on the grounds of its colonizing functions (Liebert, 2019). These arguments are at odds with some of the most fundamental principles of community psychology and social work, where this model has been extensively applied. Indeed, both disciplines prioritize the inclusion of those who have experienced social injustices and advocate for participant-driven and qualitative approaches (e.g., Kagan et al. 2022).

Perhaps most perplexing, then, is that many community psychologists have taken up this theory with such gusto. One reason may be that systems theory is often presented as atheoretical, which ignores these heavy epistemological and philosophical assumptions. For instance, it has been argued that "systems theory does not specify particular theoretical frameworks for understanding problems, and it does not direct the social worker to specific intervention strategies. Rather it serves as an organizing conceptual framework or metatheory" (Friedman & Allen, 2011, p. 3). These types of interpretations miss the point that broader conceptual frameworks and metatheories function to define the theoretical boundaries and scope of intelligibility in research and practice. Presenting systems theory as atheoretical obscures the theoretical and epistemological underpinnings that construct these boundaries. Even more alarmingly, this produces a body of knowledge and practice that is ignorant to its own theoretical groundings.

One other related reason that systems theory may have been taken up with such gusto has to do with its location and origins. Systems theory, and Bronfenbrenner's *Ecological Systems Theory* more specifically, are particularly popular in the United States, where they were developed. Within this context, it has been argued that American community psychology is particularly problematic in its largely uncritical stance and reproduction of colonial logics and modes of knowing:

> Critical community psychologists see as problematic the way that U.S. versions of community psychology colonize and potentially dilute more critical decolonizing forms of community psychology in other parts of the world, for example, in South Africa, South and Central America, New Zealand, and Australia (Duckett, 2009, Fryer & Fox, 2015, Fryer & Laing, 2008, Gridley & Breen, 2007). Community psychology is shaped by Western academic traditions that tend to reproduce historical power hierarchies intertwined with the legacy of colonialism (Reyes Cruz & Sonn, 2011).
>
> *(Evans et al. 2016, p. 114)*

The theory of *systemic trauma* is therefore problematic due to the reproduction, at its core, of dominant individualized notions and ways of knowing trauma, based on the dominant individuated concept of the self that underpins the neoliberal psychological subject (Rose, 1985). Systems theory more broadly is problematic in its reproduction of scientific methods and colonial ways of 'Knowing' (Liebert, 2019), which treat complex social relations as objective environments of exposure that 'give rise to' such trauma. And, because fundamental assumptions about the 'ecosystem' have largely been rejected, this calls into question one of the most fundamental assumptions of this theory. Coupled with a lack of critical attention to theory (including such theoretical shortcomings) in practical applications of systems theory, this leaves several questionable theoretical assumptions unexamined. And, in relation to an expanded analytic of trauma, while 'systemic trauma' invokes institutions in order to understand experiences of trauma, systems theory is limited in terms of its focus on the individual as the site for trauma and its management. This means – again – that responses to trauma are typically leveled at individuals rather than institutions. So, while the theory of systemic trauma rightfully identifies the importance of institutional conditions in (re)productions of trauma, systems theory may not be the most useful way to explain this.

This prompts the most pressing question of this book: What does it mean to have an institutional analytic of trauma that takes institutions as the primary site of intervention and transformation?

Institutional Trauma: Trauma as a Product of Institutional Power

In order to understand and address the profound entanglements of institutions and trauma, we must understand institutions not only as environments and settings, but also as "a complex of relations forming part of the ruling apparatus, organized around a distinctive function–education, health care, law, and the like" (Smith, 1987, p. 160). For instance, feminist perspectives have introduced politicized readings of trauma as a form of dominance, emphasizing the role of power in shaping how trauma is experienced and understood (Griffiths, 2018). Now, I will offer an institutional analytic of trauma based on three foundational claims that take institutions as sites of intervention and transformation.

Claim 1: Institutions Are Methods for the (re)production of Trauma and Can Be Conceptualized on This Basis

The first claim is that institutions are methods for the (re)production of trauma. Therefore, to address trauma, we can conceptualize institutions as methods for the (re)production of trauma on this basis. Critical trauma theorists have articulated this claim through the concept of institutional damage:

> Critical race and critical legal theorists in the United States and Europe have usefully analyzed the specific damages produced in relation to the law, prison industry and immigration policy, for example. Likewise the case of trauma that exceeds individual bodily experience is also difficult to localize and thereby normalize.
> *(Stevens, 2011, p. 179)*

Here, the observation that the experience of trauma 'exceeds individual bodily experience' and is lodged in powerful institutions explicitly constructs trauma as institutional. Institutional responses to trauma can therefore resist the standardization of trauma and address the difficulties of localization and normalization on this basis. This includes looking beyond dominant biopsychiatric theories that locate trauma in the body and normalize specific conceptualizations of trauma on this basis, and instead imagining how trauma may be institutionally produced. As I will discuss in Chapter 6, this might include *disbanding theory*, invoking *critical trauma studies*, and developing a *thick description of trauma*. In doing so, institutional responses to trauma can consider how trauma comes to be made in particular institutional realms and how to intervene in such realms.

Claim 2: Trauma Is Institutionally Specific and Situated, and Can Be Understood on This Basis

In relation to the first claim, the second claim is that experiences of and knowledge(s) about trauma and institutions are always specific and situated. Therefore, when looking at any experience of trauma, we can recognize that institutions are always implicitly and explicitly implicated in that experience and how it is understood; even in what appear to be individualized, objective explanations:

> Examining institutions of practice like clinical service provision, legal language and action, cyberspace memorializing, and popular media representations of terrorism and catastrophe can illuminate what it

means that experiences of trauma, diagnoses of PTSD, easy memorializing, bodily instruction, and even legal framings of unacceptable harm *make bodies*. Beyond that, though, undertaking these reflections can show how the work of trauma in one institutional location feeds into and draws upon its iterations in other institutions. How, for example, legal definitions of the tortured body rely on limiting concepts of physical and mental traumatic injury, which in turn, supply the logics and just cause to training institutions, cyberspatial sites of memorialization, and representations of terrorism and its effects.
(Stevens, 2011, p. 184)

Institutional responses to trauma can therefore address how institutions actively regulate understandings and experiences of trauma, and therefore traumatized subjectivities. As discussed in Chapters 2, 3, and 4, expressions and understandings of trauma are institutionally mediated by psychotherapeutic frameworks, law, medicine, media outlets, and the family, among many others, which govern how, when, and even if, trauma is and can be expressed and understood. This is how experiences of trauma become institutionally bound. Therefore, institutionally specific conceptualizations of trauma itself are critical to the project of institutional intervention. As I will discuss in Chapter 6, this might include exploring a *pattern theory of self*, generating *institutional ethnographies* of trauma, and exploring *emplacements of trauma*.

Claim 3: Trauma is an Inherent Product of Institutional Power and Can Be Resisted on This Basis

The third claim is that trauma is an inherent product of institutional power, and therefore can be resisted on this basis. This third claim recognizes that rather than constituting a rupture in an otherwise 'normal' world, trauma can be viewed as an inherent and ongoing product of institutional power. On this basis, institutional responses to trauma can resist dominant assumptions and logics of the psy disciplines, pathologizing practices, individuating ideologies, and notions of isolated incidents, in order to resist trauma itself. Rejecting the pathologizing dichotomy of 'normal' and 'abnormal' – and efforts to further pathologize trauma through expansions of diagnostic lexicons – this claim instead urges institutional resistance against pathologizing notions of trauma and imagines efforts to resist trauma against and beyond these realms.

The logic underpinning this claim is that since institutions form the grounds for profound (re)productions of trauma, they should also form the grounds of intervention and transformation. Taking just the examples discussed in Chapter 4 shows that the psy disciplines produce therapeutic harm, (neo)colonialism produces state violence, and heterogender and the family produce sexual and domestic violence, all of which are associated with trauma. This demonstrates the vast and cumulative traumatic realms of institutions beyond isolated incidents and individuals. Therefore, rather than focusing attention primarily on individual transformation, institutional responses can resist trauma by focusing primarily on institutional transformation.

Casting trauma as an inherent product of institutional power rather than an individual problem that must be fixed at the individual level therefore opens up different pathways for addressing trauma based on institutional resistance. Critical trauma theorists argue that this form of resistance can open up possibilities for embodying trauma in institutional terms:

> we can extend our notions of the body and embodiment by analyzing trauma's manifestation in clinical settings by focusing on PTSD not simply as a diagnosis, but as a set of practices that include service utilization, diagnosis, psychotropic medicating, imaging technologies, hospitalization, and efforts to revise the Diagnostic and Statistical Manual. Limiting conceptions of trauma have shaped the basic assumptions and material activities attending notions of harm, injury, and their subjects. Shifting from our conception of trauma as a descriptive term, and moving to thinking of it as a concept that makes subjects and shapes bodies through the function of significant social institutions, can help us determine and propose alternative approaches to assessing and responding to our social suffering without recourse to disavowal.
>
> *(Stevens, 2011, p. 184–185)*

This institutional reframing of trauma serves as a means of resistance against dominant notions of individual resilience and recovery in the face of trauma. As I will discuss in Chapter 6, instead of getting people 'over' trauma, institutional responses might include resistance in the form of *melancholy, psychiatric abolition,* and *justice by any means.*

Conclusion

An expanded institutional analytic of trauma can provide a powerful approach to trauma, allowing possibilities for understanding and resisting trauma on institutional grounds. In contrast with theoretical perspectives that construct trauma as 'other' to the institution, the expanded institutional analytic discussed in Chapter 4 provides a broader definition of institutions, which reveals how trauma is fundamentally made in institutions. In this chapter, I have evaluated two dominant theories, *institutional betrayal* and *systemic trauma*, in terms of the extent to which they reflect an expanded analytic of institutions. In this evaluation, I have argued that both theories are grounded in dominant assumptions about trauma, institutions, the individual, and modes of knowing that are incongruent with an expanded institutional analytic. Moreover, both theories reflect a dominating 'desire to know' (Liebert, 2019), which forecloses possibilities to explore the *negative space* surrounding dominant trauma theory. In both cases, the individual psychological subject is placed in sharp focus as the site of trauma and its management. This further strengthens the case I have made for an expanded institutional analytic, which treats institutions as sites for intervention and transformation in response to trauma. Drawing on this expanded institutional analytic, I have discussed how trauma can be viewed as a product of institutional power. In contrast with the two theories presented in the current chapter, this institutional analytic articulates trauma as made in institutional power, and views *institutions as methods* for the production of trauma. On this basis, I have offered some foundational claims that may be helpful in guiding institutional responses to trauma. In Chapter 6, I will consider a range of conceptual tools that could be taken up in response to such claims.

References

Ahmed, S. (2012). *On Being Included: Racism and Diversity in Institutional Life*. Duke University Press.

Ahn, R., Alpert, E. J., Purcell, G., Konstantopoulos, W. M., McGahan, A., Cafferty, E., Eckardt, M., Conn, K. L., Cappetta, K., & Burke, T. F. (2013). Human trafficking: review of educational resources for health professionals. *American journal of preventive medicine*, 44(3), 283–289. https://doi.org/10.1016/j.amepre.2012.10.025

Beske M. A. (2009). Applying international human rights laws to promote wellness within the community: on diminishing intimate partner violence in the context of western Belize. *Global public health*, 4(5), 490–499. https://doi.org/10.1080/17441690902815447

Bowers, N. R., & Bowers, A. (2017). General Systems Theory. In F. J. Turner (Ed.), *Social Work Treatment: Interlocking Theoretical Approaches* (pp. 240–247). Oxford University Press.

Bronfenbrenner, U. (1977). Toward an experimental ecology of human development. *American Psychologist*, 32(7), 513–531.

Casey, E. A., & Lindhorst, T. P. (2009). Toward a multi-level, ecological approach to the primary prevention of sexual assault: prevention in peer and community contexts. *Trauma, violence & abuse, 10(2)*, 91–114. https://doi.org/10.1177/1524838009334129

Curtis, A. (2011a, May 30). *The Use and Abuse of Vegetational Concepts* [Broadcast]. British Broadcasting Corporation.

Curtis, A. (2011b, May 28). *How the "ecosystem" myth has been used for sinister means*. https://www.theguardian.com/environment/2011/may/29/adam-curtis-ecosystems-tansley-smuts

Duckett, P. (2009). Critical reflections on key community psychology concepts: Off-setting our capitalist emissions? *Forum Gemeindepsychologie, 14(2)*. http://www.gemeindepsychologie.de/fg-2-2009_06.html

Evans, S. D., Duckett, P., Lawthom, R., & Kivell, N. (2016). Positioning the Critical in Community Psychology. In *APA Handbook of Community Psychology: Theoretical Foundations, Core Concepts, and Emerging Challenges*. (pp. 107–127). American Psychological Association.

Filippaki, I., & Salter, M. (2021). Trauma, narratives, institutions: Transdisciplinary dialogs. *Journal of Trauma and Dissociation, 22*(4), 407–412. https://doi.org/10.1080/15299732.2021.1925861

Freyd, J. J., (1994). Betrayal trauma: Traumatic amnesia as an adaptive response to childhood abuse. *Ethics & Behavior, 4*(4), 307–329. https://doi.org/https://doi.org/10.1207/s15327019eb0404_1

Freyd, J. J., Klest, B., & Allard, C. B. (2005). Betrayal trauma: relationship to physical health, psychological distress, and a written disclosure intervention. *Journal of Trauma & Dissociation, 6*(3), 83–104. https://doi.org/10.1300/J229v06n03_04

Friedman, B. D., & Allen, K. N. (2011). Systems Theory. In J. R. Brandell (Ed.), *Theory & Practice in Clinical Social Work* (2nd ed., pp. 3–20). Sage Publications, Inc.

Fryer, D., & Fox, R. (2015). Community psychology: Subjectivity, power, collectivity. In I. Parker (Ed.), *Handbook of critical psychology* (pp. 145–154). Routledge.

Fryer, D., & Laing, A. (2008). Community Psychologies: What are they? What could they be? Why does it matter? A Critical Community Psychology Approach. *Australian Community Psychologist, 20*(2), 7–15.

Gallagher, S. (2013). A pattern theory of self. *Frontiers in Human Neuroscience*, 7, 1–7. https://doi.org/10.3389/fnhum.2013.00443

Gergen, K. (1971). *The Concept of Self*. Holt, Rinehart and Winston, Inc.

Gergen, K. J. (2015). *An Invitation to Social Construction* (3rd ed.). Sage Publications Ltd.

Goldsmith, R. E., Martin, C. G., & Smith, C. P. (2014). Systemic Trauma. *Journal of Trauma and Dissociation, 15*(2), 117–132. https://doi.org/10.1080/15299732.2014.871666

Gough, B., McFadden, M., & McDonald, M. (2013). *Critical Social Psychology: An Introduction*. Palgrave Macmillan.

Grant, M. M., Cannistraci, C., Hollon, S. D., Gore, J., & Shelton, R. (2011). Childhood trauma history differentiates amygdala response to sad faces within MDD. *Journal of Psychiatric Research, 45*(7), 886–895. https://doi.org/10.1016/j.jpsychires.2010.12.004

Gridley, H., & Breen, L. J. (2007). So far and yet so near? Community psychology in Australia. In S. Reich, M. Riemer, I. Prilleltensky, & M. Montero (Eds.), *International community psychology: History and theories* (1st ed., pp. 119–139). http://dx.doi.org/10.1007/978-0-387-49500-2_6

Griffiths, J. (2018). Feminist Interventions in Trauma Studies. In J. R. Kurtz (Ed.), *Trauma and Literature* (pp. 181–195). Cambridge University Press.

Haines, S. K. (2019). *The Politics of Trauma: Somatics, Healing, and Social Justice*. North Atlantic Books.

Hatcher, A. M., Romito, P., Odero, M., Bukusi, E. A., Onono, M., & Turan, J. M. (2013). Social context and drivers of intimate partner violence in rural Kenya: implications for the health of pregnant women. *Culture, Health & Sexuality, 15*(4), 404–419. https://doi.org/10.1080/13691058.2012.760205

Healy, K. (2012). Remembering, apologies, and truth: Challenges for social work today. *Australian Social Work, 65*(3), 288–294. https://doi.org/10.1080/0312407X.2012.705308

Herman, J. L. (1992). *Trauma and Recovery*. Basic Books.

Hornstein, G. A. (2013). Whose account matters? A challenge to feminist psychologists. *Feminism & Psychology, 23*(1), 29–40. https://doi.org/10.1177/0959353512467964

Kagan, C., Akhurst, J., Alfaro, J., Lawthom, R., Richards, M., & Zambrano, A. (2022). *The Routledge International Handbook of Community Psychology: Facing Global Crises with Hope*. Routledge.

Khúc, M. (2024). *dear elia: Letters from the Asian American Abyss*. Duke University Press.

Liebert, R. J. (2019). *Psycurity*. Routledge.

Lilienfield, R. (1978). *The Rise of Systems Theory: An Ideological Analysis*. John Wiley & Sons, Inc.

Lucero, N. M., & Bussey, M. (2012). A collaborative and trauma-informed practice model for urban Indian child welfare. *Child Welfare, 91*(3), 89–112.

Newman, L. (2013). Seeking Asylum—Trauma, Mental Health, and Human Rights: An Australian Perspective. *Journal of Trauma & Dissociation, 14*(2), 213–223. https://doi.org/10.1080/15299732.2013.724342

O'Brien, B. S., & Sher, L. (2013). Military sexual trauma as a determinant in the development of mental and physical illness in male and female veterans. *International Journal of Adolescent Medicine and Health, 25*(3), 269–274. https://doi.org/10.1515/ijamh-2013-0061

O'Neill, E. (n.d.). *Cybernetic Emigres: Wartime Machines and the Problem of Life between Vienna and the United States*. Botstiber Institute for Austrian-American Studies. Retrieved May 19, 2024, from https://botstiberbiaas.org/cybernetic-emigres-wartime-machines-and-the-problem-of-life-between-vienna-and-the-united-states/

Potter, J. (1996). *Representing Reality: Discourse, Rhetoric and Social Construction*. SAGE Publications Ltd.

Ray, S. L. (2008). Trauma from a global perspective. *Issues in Mental Health Nursing, 29*(1), 63–72. https://doi.org/10.1080/01612840701748821

Reilly, J. M., & Gravdal, J. A. (2012). An ecological model for family violence prevention across the life cycle. *Family Medicine, 44*(5), 332–335.

Reyes Cruz, M., & Sonn, C. C. (2011). (De)colonizing culture in community psychology: reflections from critical social science. *American journal of community psychology, 47(1–2)*, 203–214. https://doi.org/10.1007/s10464-010-9378-x

Rose, N. (1985). *The Psychological Complex: Psychology, Politics and Society in England, 1869–1939.* Routledge & Kegan Paul.

Smith, C. P., & Freyd, J. J. (2014). Institutional betrayal. *American Psychologist, 69*(6), 575–584. https://doi.org/10.1037/a0037564

Smith, D. E. (1987). *The Everyday World as Problematic: A Feminist Sociology.* Northeastern University Press.

Smith, R. D. (2021). Toward a theory of institutions: Institutional betrayal and dispersions of accountability at Johns Hopkins University. *Journal of Trauma and Dissociation, 22*(4), 465–477. https://doi.org/10.1080/15299732.2021.1925867

Stevens, M. E. (2011). Trauma's Essential Bodies. In M. J. Casper & P. Currah (Eds.), *Corpus: An Interdisciplinary Reader on Bodies and Knowledge* (pp. 171–186). Palgrave Macmillan.

Subica, A. M., Claypoole, K. H., & Wylie, A. M. (2012). PTSD'S mediation of the relationships between trauma, depression, substance abuse, mental health, and physical health in individuals with severe mental illness: evaluating a comprehensive model. *Schizophrenia Research, 136(1–3)*, 104–109. https://doi.org/10.1016/j.schres.2011.10.018

Thompson, L. (2021). Toward a feminist psychological theory of "institutional trauma." *Feminism & Psychology, 31*(1), 99–118. https://doi.org/10.1177/0959353520968374

Tseris, E. (2019). Social work and women's mental health: Does trauma theory provide a useful framework? *British Journal of Social Work, 49(3)*, 686–703. https://doi.org/10.1093/bjsw/bcy090

Wiener, N. (1948). *Cybernetics: Or Control and Communication in the Animal and the Machine.* The Technology Press.

Wiener, N. (1961). *Cybernetics: Or Control and Communication in the Animal and the Machine* (2nd ed.). The MIT Press.

6
(DE)THEORIZING AND (RE)IMAGINING INSTITUTIONAL TRAUMA

Introduction

In Chapter 4, I promised to return to the following question:

> What could histories of psychology that foreground other-than-Enlightenment—that is, based on Eurocentric White male, Cartesian dualist—rationality, for example, look like? What other actors, experiences, knowledges, feelings, and practices might become central, and how might historians need to engage in new praxes to think, write, and feel with—rather than about—their subjects?
> *(Bhatia et al. 2023, p. 62)*

In this chapter, I will expand on this question, applying the expanded institutional analytic developed in Chapters 4 and 5 to develop a response to trauma based on other 'actors, experiences, knowledges, feelings, and practices'. Guided by a recognition of the dominant Euro-American trauma concept as a "neo-colonial imposition" that functions to marginalize and silence localized understandings and responses to distress (Segalo, 2015, p. 447), I will imagine what an expanded institutional analytic of trauma can bring into view, moving beyond dominant assumptions about the boundaries of individuals, trauma, and institutions. This will involve looking at trauma beyond medicalized frameworks and individual symptoms, with a specific focus on institutions. The goal here is not to lay claim to trauma by solidifying a new scientific theory or way of knowing: This would simply reproduce scientific modes of 'Knowing' that serve to colonize experience, the mind, and the self (Liebert, 2019, p. 12). Rather, this is an invitation to explore what I refer to as the *negative space* surrounding trauma and imagine how we can approach trauma outside of dominant conceptualizations.

DOI: 10.4324/9781003042471-6

To do this, I will invoke a range of conceptual tools that can bring the institutional realms of trauma into view and allow for institutional intervention and transformation. These are by no means comprehensive, and nor should they be. Rather, they serve as examples that can be invoked in order to bring institutions into focus. As such, these examples constitute ways into the negative space surrounding dominant conceptualizations of trauma, rather than an attempt to curtail it.

Claim 1: Institutions Are Methods for the (re)production of Trauma and Can Be Conceptualized on This Basis

The first claim I outlined in Chapter 5 invites understandings of institutions as methods for the (re)production of trauma based on an expanded analytic of institutions. This can be imagined as the *negative space* around dominant realist understandings of institutions. Specifically, this claim views institutions as methods for the (re)production of knowledge about trauma, which then informs specific kinds of action in response to trauma. The conceptual tools I discuss here bring institutions into focus as methods for this (re)production of knowledge and action and locate institutions as sites for intervention and transformation on this basis. These tools come in the form of *disbanding theory*, *critical trauma studies*, and a *thick description of trauma*.

Disbanding Theory

The first conceptual tool that may be invoked in response to the first claim is the practice of *disbanding theory* – or – engaging in the process of de-theorizing. This conceptual tool invites intervention in the pace, determination, and mode of the psy disciplines to 'Know' trauma. This is again grounded in the observation that the dominant Euro-American trauma concept is a "neo-colonial imposition" (Segalo, 2015, p. 447). In her "critical psychological response to contemporary conditions of white supremacy" (p. 11), Liebert (2019) articulates the practice of psychological theorizing as a mode of coloniality:

> the West's intellectuals mapped the idea of order onto 'natural laws' – freeing the 'objective set of facts' into something 'out there,' repressing any recognition of social reality being locally, collectively produced. Now seen in universal terms, the world as an entirety became Knowable.
>
> *(Liebert, 2019, p. 78)*

In this work, Liebert (2019) gives shape to the workings of white supremacy via psychology. Here, she locates Science's *desire to know* in a colonial "fear-of-regressing" (p. 85). Driven by paranoia, this *desire to know* operates through impositions of colonial modes of rationality, prediction, and control, and the othering of the 'abnormal.' As such, "... paranoia's predicting enables both a 'statement of fact' and 'quantification' – speaking and knowing with certainty, asserting reality as if there were no other, and turning one's future into formula" (Liebert, 2019, p. 91). Such certainty, it is argued, requires *epistemologies of ignorance* (Alcoff, 2007). Indeed, as Liebert (2019) observes, "the hierarchy of Knowing, Knowers, Knowledge depends on an ignoring of worldly vitality, Indigenous capacity, colonial violence, the primordial unknown, and white supremacy" (Liebert, 2019, p. 83).

Invoking Sylvia Wynter's conceptualization of *de-supernaturalizing* (Wynter, 2003) as the process by which the unknown and the 'Other' were obliterated in service to coloniality, Liebert (2019) argues that "this new mode of Knowing required the making, disregarding, and exterminating of a physical referent for its irrational or sub-rational other" (p. 79). This involved Science (with a capital S) – including social science – "staking a territory" (Liebert, 2019, p. 103) on being, subjectivity, and the psyche, and foreclosing imagination otherwise. Indeed, as Liebert observes, "positivist yearning requires not just an ignorance but a destruction of other possible worlds" (Liebert, 2019, p. 82). Such a *desire to know* "blocks, refuses, ignores other worlds" (Liebert, 2019, p. 110). As discussed in Chapter 4, it was this colonial foreclosure that underpinned the development of the psychological subject:

> it was people's capacities as healers, sorcerers, and performers of incantations and divinations that were persecuted during the witch-hunts; capacities that enacted the liveliness of the land, the non-linearity of time, and the relationality of ourselves. In order to dominate it, capitalism required that the world be disenchanted and the abilities of the body to tune into this vitality – capacities embraced by witches – be exorcised. Alienated, this new Cartesian body was treated as a machine, as brute matter disconnected from knowing, wanting, feeling. Making its operations intelligible and controllable; constructing the prototypical individual with which Psychology is built and builds.
>
> *(Liebert, 2019, p. 7)*

Citing Eve Kosofsky Sedgwick's reading of paranoia (Sedgwick, 2003), Liebert (2019) observes that:

> As opposed to the 'strong theory' of paranoid readings, so weighty it can't be moved, she suggests experimenting with 'weak theory', with making multiple, localized, unstable knowledges that – welcoming surprise and organized with hope – do justice to a wider affective range.
> *(Liebert, 2019, p. 96)*

This includes a departure from dominant psychological knowledge, which extends even to the conceptualization of the 'real' in Western intellectual realism and constructions of 'objective' reality. Indeed, in what world is human distress simply knowable through observed behaviors or symptoms, as positivism and empiricism imagine? Here we can again invoke Kriss (2013) who explicates how ignorance flows through such views, reminding us that:

> DSM-5 describes a nightmare society in which human beings are individuated, sick, and alone. For much of the novel, what the narrator of this story is describing is its own solitude, its own inability to appreciate other people, and its own overpowering desire for death—but the real horror lies in the world that could produce such a voice.
> *(Kriss, 2013, para 15)*

Focusing instead on 'weak theory,' Liebert (2019) conjures magic, mystery, hope, surprise, and imagination as forms of decolonizing. For "mystery offers to breathe new life into a space" (Liebert, 2019, p. 122) and enables decolonizing through "discomfort from that present colonial past of hunting and burning, diagnosing and treating, as though we Know" (p. 122):

> To admit magic is to surrender to not Knowing, to things not being Knowable; an admission necessary for imagination.
> *(Liebert, 2019, p. 121)*

'Weak' theory disbands that which is immovable by generating multiple, localized, unstable knowledges instead. In doing so, 'weak' theory opens up the negative space of trauma against an immovable foreground of dominant knowledge, and the role of the psy disciplines and (neo)coloniality in the generation of such knowledge. Thus, 'weak' theory reveals the psy disciplines as methods for the (re)production of dominant ways of knowing and understanding trauma, and offers an analytical tool that can be taken up in response to disband theory beyond dominant assumptions, ways of knowing, and the colonial *desire to know*. To an extent, Chapters 2 and 3 have engaged in this process by recognizing how the institutional production of knowledge about trauma has constrained knowledge about trauma, and opening this up to questioning. As such, the institutional bounding of the ways that trauma can be imagined is treated as the site of intervention and transformation here. But this practice does more than reveal the workings of institutions: It also invites us to imagine trauma outside of the bounds of Knowing that foreclose such imagination.

Critical Trauma Studies

The second conceptual tool that may be invoked in response to the first claim is *critical trauma studies*. I have invoked critical trauma studies throughout this book in stark contrast with dominant trauma theories, primarily through the work of Maurice E. Stevens (2011, 2016), bringing this in and out of focus as I have switched between the foreground of the psy disciplines and the *negative space* of trauma. In doing so, my goal has been to show how, just as with visual images that deploy negative space, the same subject can be viewed entirely differently depending on one's focus.

The area of critical trauma studies offers a reorientation of trauma in response to theoretical and epistemic domination. Like the practice of *disbanding theory*, this analytic brings trauma into focus as a cultural object, thereby lodging understandings of trauma in institutional realms. Speaking of the epistemological shift brought about by critical trauma studies, Wertheimer and Casper (2016) observe a reframing of trauma, "recognizing and naming "trauma" not only as a condition of broken bodies and shattered minds, but also and primarily as a cultural object. In these framings, "trauma" is a product of history and politics, subject to reinterpretation, contestation, and intervention" (p. 3). As discussed in Chapter 1, this epistemological shift aligns with critical psychological perspectives, which are concerned with the constructions and representations of phenomena that give them their meaning and invite or warrant particular forms of action. Therefore, rather than taking 'trauma' for granted, or at face value, critical trauma studies examines the production of knowledge about trauma, how this is taken up, and what other meanings or assumptions make this possible:

> Critical trauma studies asks: What does it mean to use the discourse of trauma? To represent events as ruptures, breaks, and other deviations from the normal? And what, then, is the normal?
> *(Wertheimer & Casper, 2016, p. 3)*

In doing so, critical trauma studies imagines trauma in a range of ways while recognizing tensions in how certain modes of knowing reflect institutional dominance or will. For instance, speaking on this tension in relation to what can be understood as the culture of 'neuroenchantment' (Ali et al. 2014), which was discussed in Chapter 2, Wertheimer and Casper (2016) observe that:

> An important task for critical trauma studies is to learn from and make use of these neuroscientific "findings", while also interrogating how neuro-stories are rapidly becoming hegemonic explanations and depictions of human life.
> *(Wertheimer & Casper, 2016, p. 5)*

Herein lies one important demarcation between critical trauma studies and the dominant psy disciplines: Critical trauma studies does not encourage the uncritical acceptance of dominant conceptualizations of trauma as 'truth,' and recommend action accordingly. Instead, critical trauma studies recognizes that trauma is an institutionally produced category of knowledge that functions to bind and define experiences based on specific cultural notions of 'normality' and 'abnormality,' and invites critical forms of intervention in response:

> Whereas clinical and psychological perspectives respond to trauma as a psychic and/or embodied marker of disruptive experience, a critical approach attends to the ways that the category of "trauma" reveals and unsettles social and cultural classification systems, including how we triage subjects for "help" and intervention.
> *(Wertheimer & Casper, 2016, p. 5–6)*

This comparison lays out the fundamental differences between responses to trauma in the dominant psy disciplines and critical trauma studies. Here, critical trauma studies explicitly recognizes that dominant psychiatric paradigms are prone to targeting the individual subject as the site for intervention, 'help,' and transformation in response to trauma. In contrast, a critical approach turns attention to the social and cultural classification systems that operate to accomplish this. And, by explicitly naming the psy disciplines, institutions – not individuals – are imagined as the site of intervention and transformation in response to trauma. This returns us to the epistemic reframing of critical trauma studies, where 'trauma' is viewed as "a product of history and politics, subject to reinterpretation, contestation, and intervention" (Wertheimer & Casper, 2016, p. 3).

Thick Description of Trauma

The third conceptual tool that may be invoked in response to the first claim is *thick description*. Thick description is commonly associated with philosopher Gilbert Ryle and anthropologist Clifford Geertz. This analytic grew specifically out of resistance against the universalizing claims and theories of positivist and empirical science, which functioned to impose what Liebert (2019, p. 117) refers to as a colonial "think-net" over phenomena. Geertz (1973) explicitly named the role of science and scientists in the production and regulation of knowledge about phenomena, explicitly stating:

> if you want to understand what a science is, you should look in the first instance not at its theories or its findings, and certainly not at what its apologists say about it; you should look at what the practitioners of it do.
>
> *(Geertz, 1973, p. 5)*

Here, practices of institutional knowledge production – especially scientific theories and ways of knowing – are imagined as the primary sites of interrogation. Speaking of such theories and ways of knowing, Geertz (1973) observes:

> they resolve so many fundamental problems at once that they seem also to promise that they will resolve all fundamental problems, clarify all obscure issues. Everyone snaps them up as the open sesame of some new positive science, the conceptual center-point around which a comprehensive system of analysis can be built. The sudden vogue of such a *grande idée*, crowding out almost everything else for a while…
>
> *(Geertz, 1973, p. 3)*

Against this, Geertz (1973) argues against 'Knowing,' observing this as an impossibility in the sense that culture and phenomena are never fully knowable. Therefore, interpretations are always incomplete. On this basis, Geertz (1973) observes that "cultural analysis is (or should be) guessing at meanings, assessing the guesses, and drawing explanatory conclusions from the better guesses, not discovering the Continent of Meaning and mapping out its bodiless landscape" (p. 20). This is in stark contrast with the certainty of positivist and empirical science:

> Cultural analysis is intrinsically incomplete. And, worse than that, the more deeply it goes the less complete it is. It is a strange science

whose most telling assertions are its most tremulously based, in which to get somewhere with the matter at hand is to intensify the suspicion, both your own and that of others, that you are not quite getting it right.

(Geertz, 1973, p. 29)

In doing so, Geertz argues against experimental science, articulating cultural inquiry as "not an experimental science in search of law but an interpretive one in search of meaning" (p. 5). To guide this 'search for meaning,' Geertz (1973) articulates the ethnographic method of thick description. Thick description, argues Geertz, is focused on the "role of culture in the construction of collective life" (p. 28). At its core, then, thick description is both a form of resistance against the scientific *desire to know* and a way to imagine experiences as complex and made in culture.

In feminist psychological research, the concept of thick description has been applied to develop rich descriptions of concepts within the realms of social and institutional conditions, thereby lodging such concepts in these conditions. For instance, in their work on sexual desire – which outlined the concept of 'thick desire' – Fine and McClelland (2006) explain that:

A framework of thick desire situates sexual well being within structural contexts that enable economic, educational, social, and psychological health... we seek to understand how laws, public policies, and institutions today both nourish and threaten young women's sense of economic, social, and sexual possibility.

(Fine & McClelland, 2006, p. 301)

In qualitative research, it has been argued that "thick description refers to giving a thorough account of the participants' views, intents, circumstances, motives, meanings, and understandings" (Younas et al., 2023, p. 1). This includes understanding the accounts given by participants in a multitude of ways. Younas et al. (2023) propose a framework for the interpretation of these multiple understandings, or narratives, of experience. In their MIRACLE framework, the authors outline seven different narratives that might be developed around participants' accounts of experience. Recognizing that such narratives are always the consequence of active interpretation, the authors identify *meaningful, interpretative, relational, authentic, contextualized, linked,* and *emic* narratives (Younas et al., 2023). The meaningful narrative centers participant understandings of their own experience, whereas the interpretative narrative centers the researcher's interpretations. The relational narrative makes space to understand the individual experience *in relation to* relationships and socio-cultural conditions and practices. The authentic narrative grounds interpretations in the participant's viewpoints. The linked narrative connects the account to broader knowledge about the experience or phenomenon, and the emic narrative situates participant accounts in relation to broader culture, social community, and other participants "based on the notion that members of the same community can discuss the same topics in different ways… and that their experiences evolve in response to their sociocultural contexts" (Younas et al., 2023, p. 6).

Thick description can also specifically be applied to considerations of trauma. The notion of *thick desire* (Fine & McClelland, 2006) can serve as a conceptual model here. On these grounds, we can imagine a thick description of trauma that accounts for social and institutional conditions, thereby lodging the concept of trauma in institutional conditions. In addition, when considering experiences of trauma, the interpretations of experts – whether these are researchers or practitioners – usually take precedence in explanations of trauma. A thick description would incorporate a range of narrative interpretations. In addition, a thick description considers the relational and institutional dynamics of that experience, meaning that trauma could be understood relationally and institutionally. A thick description therefore enables an account of trauma that is made in institutional realms and dynamics, including the interpretative frameworks of those experiencing it. It is precisely through this focus on institutional realms and dynamics that thick description brings institutions into view as sites of intervention and transformation.

Claim 2: Trauma Is Institutionally Specific and Situated, and Can Be Understood on This Basis

Having considered how we can understand institutions as methods for the (re)production of trauma, the second claim turns our attention to the specificity of understandings and experiences of trauma on this basis. This follows Segalo's articulation of the need to generate localized and situated understandings of trauma (Segalo, 2015). Against the universalizing claims of dominant theories (see Chapter 2), this claim invites an explicit recognition of specificity in order to understand and respond to trauma as institutionally specific and situated. The conceptual tools I discuss here therefore imagine ways to reinhabit and respond to trauma as partial, specific, and situated. These tools come in the form of a *pattern theory of self*, *institutional ethnographies*, and *emplacements of trauma*.

Pattern Theory of Self

The first conceptual tool that may be invoked in response to this second claim is a *pattern theory of self*. Originating in neuroscience, I invoke this tool generally to demonstrate that critical, complex, situated notions of selfhood can be imagined in even the most dominant disciplines of trauma knowledge production. This tool is also invoked specifically in response to Nikolas Rose's consideration of the psychological subject and its accompanying presumptions (see Chapter 2). Such a consideration reveals how the self has primarily been construed on individualized terms within the psy disciplines. For Henriques et al. (1984), the 'subject' has been used as code for the 'individual' in psychology, subsuming subjectivity under individualism and leading to what has been termed 'individual-society dualism' (Henriques et al. 1984). This mode of selfhood has been invoked in understandings of trauma, which hinge on notions of the individual psychological subject. As discussed in Chapter 3, this mode of selfhood functions to cast trauma into individuals, who are imagined outside of the broader institutions that give experiences and understandings of trauma their shape and meaning. On this basis, an expanded institutional analytic of trauma requires a conceptualization of selfhood that can be located and situated in institutional realms.

A pattern theory of self allows for an imagination of a self beyond the individualism of the dominant psy disciplines. Here, selfhood is viewed as inseparable from broader socio-political conditions, and cultural construals of selfhood themselves. In contrast with the broadly individuating approach of the psy disciplines, Gallagher (2013) proposes the *pattern theory of self*, wherein "a self is constituted by a number of characteristic features or aspects that may include minimal embodied, minimal experiential, affective, intersubjective, psychological/cognitive, narrative, extended, and situated aspects" (p. 1). This conceptualization of selfhood in multitudes bridges individual-society dualism, and expands the realms of possibility for imagining a self beyond dominant modes of thought in the psy disciplines. Indeed, such multitudes are viewed as compatible rather than oppositional (Gallagher, 2013). In addition, the assertion that "any claim to explain something called 'the self' immediately raises a host of problems" (Gallagher, 2013, p. 1), acts as a problematization of the certainty of coloniality (Liebert, 2019). The pattern theory of self responds with a complex notion of selfhood wherein universalizing notions of the self are rejected:

> what we call self consists of a complex and sufficient pattern of certain contributories, none of which on their own is necessary or

essential to any particular self. This is not a pattern theory of "*the self*". Rather, what we call "self" is a cluster concept which includes a sufficient number of characteristic features. Taken together, a certain pattern of characteristic features constitute an individual self.

(Gallagher, 2013, p. 3)

Here, selfhood "is not a fixed entity but is rather an ongoing production which brings a real but contingent coherence to an evolving (or in some cases, devolving) stream of sensations, thoughts, emotions, desires, memories, and anticipations" (Gallagher & Daly, 2018, p. 1). This opens possibilities to imagine selfhood as situated, contingent, and inextricable from the worlds that give it meaning:

> selves are only ever apprehended as immersed in a meaningful world; it accommodates change and adaptation to context; and at the same time it acknowledges a coherent organization as the locus of experience and self-ascription. On this account, dynamical self-patterns involve and are revealed in self-narratives, which track regenerative self-organizing processes.
>
> *(Gallagher & Daly, 2018, p. 1)*

While the pattern theory of self invokes some of the most dominant neuroscientific and cognitivist assertions within and beyond the domain of trauma studies, it also deconstructs the central presumption of individualism that underpins notions of selfhood in these domains. This is important, especially in relation to such dominant assertions. Because this central mode of understanding selfhood functions to cast trauma into individuals, a pattern theory of self offers ways to imagine selfhood otherwise. Specifically, the focus of pattern theory on self-in-context allows for imaginations of selfhood that are situated in broader specific institutional conditions and relations, thereby enabling understandings of selfhood as institutionally produced, and a self that is institutionally specific. On this basis, pattern theory supports an expanded institutional analytic of trauma that can imagine traumatized selfhood in institutional realms and imagine institutions as sites for intervention and transformation on this basis.

Institutional Ethnographies

The second conceptual tool that may be invoked in response to the second claim is *institutional ethnographies*. Institutional ethnographies get at institutional specificities by generating localized knowledge(s) that do not aim to colonize experience but instead generate new forms of imagination. In line with Segalo (2015), this allows for the generation of localized understandings and responses to distress, which have been obscured by dominant trauma theory. Indeed, as discussed in Chapter 4, just as institutions can be viewed as 'feminist pedagogy' (Ahmed, 2017), institutions can be viewed as 'trauma pedagogy' in the sense that we learn about trauma through institutional experiences.

As discussed in Chapter 4, this begins with the observation that institutions can be understood as social, ideological, and discursive arrangements, and Dorothy E. Smith's definition of institutions as "a complex of relations forming part of the ruling apparatus, organized around a distinctive function–education, health care, law, and the like" (Smith, 1987, p. 160). Taken from this perspective, institutions can be viewed as arbiters of dominant ideologies, social orders, relations, and practices. Institutional ethnographies bring such institutional realms squarely into the 'frame of analysis' (Ahmed, 2012, p. 21) by examining the social relations that operate on the particular experience or phenomenon in question (Smith & Griffith, 2022).

As I have argued before, ethnographic, autoethnographic, and ethnomethodological approaches allow for the development of institutionally situated accounts of experiences and shared social realities of trauma (Thompson, 2021). This is because "an explicit attention to institutions teaches us about their implicit significance and meaning" (Ahmed, 2012, p. 22). This attention can take endless forms. Indeed, in what can be understood as a direct resistance against the "think-net" (Liebert, 2019, p. 117), Smith's opening statement in *Institutional Ethnography as Practice* reminds the reader: "THIS BOOK IS NOT A MANUAL: it is not a 'how-to-do-it' collection that will give you all the answers, tell you exactly how to produce a piece of research that others can recognize as institutional ethnography, solve all the problems you run into in doing and writing up your ethnographic research, or otherwise provide you with models with which you can bring your work into conformity." (Smith, 2006, p. 1).

Its location in the domain of sociology has undoubtedly cast institutional ethnography as irrelevant to the mainstream psy disciplines. However, an expanded institutional analytic of trauma requires ways to engage with institutions, and, more specifically, the role of institutions in situating and giving specific shape and meanings to experiences of trauma. For example, an experience of trauma that is viewed and treated through the psy disciplines is given its shape and meaning by the meanings and practices inherent to this institutional domain. Similarly, when trauma is treated as a consequence of violence, the conditions and relations that make that violence possible give trauma its shape and meaning. And, for those who are met with individualizing responses to such experiences, it can be frustrating to have these conditions ignored. Indeed, in my engagement with support in these realms, individual level interventions left me perplexed about why I was being constructed as the problem in need of fixing, when so much of my problem was with institutions.

Institutional ethnography levels attention at institutions as sites for intervention and transformation. Examining how institutions coordinate and organize ruling relations can open up possibilities to identify how these specific ruling relations work in any given institutional domain, and understand the consequences of these ruling relations, including trauma, on this basis. As such, "institutional ethnography's project of inquiry and discovery rejects the dominance of theory" (Smith, 2005, p. 49). Instead, localized understandings are generated through institutional examination. In the case of trauma, this could include examining how trauma is institutionally defined, experienced, and (re)produced either individually or collectively. Here, institutional ethnography opens up possibilities to intervene in and transform ruling relations, and institutions as a vehicle for these. This generation of local knowledge allows for a kind of specificity that universalizing theories do not, enabling localized, situated, and specific understandings of – and responses to – trauma. Here, institutions are treated as sites of intervention and transformation.

Emplacements of Trauma

The third conceptual tool that may be invoked in response to the second claim is *emplacements of trauma*. This geographical analytic recognizes that "conceptions and practices of trauma are imbued with geopolitics" (Ehrkamp et al. 2022, p. 717), and lodged in "displacement, emplacement, and transitivity" (Ehrkamp et al. 2022, p. 715). In their large-scale qualitative research tracing the mobilization of trauma concepts and practices in processes of refugee resettlement, the authors argue that due to the level of 'tremendous flux and uncertainty' in such conditions, "trauma is neither a one-time event that is endlessly relived and reactivated in identical episodes nor does trauma emplace a singular geography. Rather, trauma can be understood as a set of serial emplacements and displacements across multiple sites" (Ehrkamp et al. 2022, p. 715). In this work, the authors document an "invidious cycle of donors in the Global North issuing calls to fund certain kinds of services" (Ehrkamp et al. 2022, p. 719) that function to shape the bounds of intelligibility for understanding and responding to trauma. Here, they describe what can be understood as a form of diagnostic imperialism:

> This discursive emplacement at the scale of individual body-minds and spaces can be recognized as part of a militarized, geopolitical imagination that works to exert sovereign boundaries and singularly narrate how humans respond to atrocity and distress.
>
> *(Ehrkamp et al. 2022, p. 720)*

Drawing on critical trauma studies, the authors turn to the notion of emplacements of trauma to develop a critique of the dominant conceptualizations of trauma underpinning such services, both in terms of the individualized theories of the psy disciplines, and the inadequacy of such theoretical frameworks outside of their own cultural specificity:

> This framework has been widely criticized for its individualized as opposed to structural focus; its attention to singular events rather than sustained, even multigenerational, suffering; and inappropriateness of its diagnoses and remedies to non-Western cultures and places.
>
> *(Ehrkamp et al. 2022, p. 715)*

This simultaneously enables possibilities to identify the cultural specificities of dominant frameworks of trauma knowledge, and a need to develop localized understandings in response. The authors draw on the concept of *geotrauma*, which locates the "temporal and spatial aspects of trauma" (Pain, 2021, p. 972) to conceptualize the specificity of trauma as "located not only within people's minds and bodies, but in the social, environmental and structural contexts around us" (Pain, 2021, p. 974). In this institutional reading of trauma, they show how trauma becomes a device for social order and control, arguing that "mental health care for trauma and other distress becomes part of refugee containment" (Ehrkamp et al. 2022, p. 716). In doing so, they theorize *trauma in geography*, locating trauma as institutionally situated, contingent, and specific:

> A growing body of work in geography has explored the multiple spatialities and emplacements of trauma, from place destruction to colonial occupation, human migration, militarism, and everyday forms of violence.
>
> *(Ehrkamp et al. 2022, p. 716)*

This geopolitical analytic "refutes the notion that trauma inheres in a person or group" (Ehrkamp et al. 2022, p. 720). As part of a broader institutional analytic of trauma, this can enable the development of institutional understandings of trauma as situated within specific global, national and/or local conditions. In turn, this can open possibilities to imagine trauma not only as inextricable from but also made by such conditions in specific ways. Doing so allows for imaginings of trauma in place, as a part of the order of things. This brings such conditions into view as sites for intervention and transformation. But this kind of imagining also does something else. Indeed, as Ehrkamp et al. (2022) observe, locating trauma as emplaced challenges dominant assumptions that trauma is an exception or aberration in an otherwise normal life:

> We see a parallel between Western constructions of trauma and population displacement in that each phenomenon continues to be framed as a rupture or exception when both are widely, if differentially, experienced.
>
> *(Ehrkamp et al. 2022, p. 715–716)*

This brings us to the third claim of this expanded institutional analytic, which allows for an understanding of trauma as an inherent product of institutional power, and encourages resistance on this basis.

Claim 3: Trauma Is an Inherent Product of Institutional Power and Can Be Resisted on This Basis

The third claim guiding this institutional analytic is that trauma is an inherent product of institutional power and can be resisted on this basis. This third claim recognizes (against epistemologies of ignorance) that rather than constituting a rupture in an otherwise 'normal' world, trauma can be viewed as an inherent and ongoing product of institutional power:

> it is the commonness of experiences of gender-based, racist and homophobic violence that challenges assumptions of cohesion or security before or after trauma.
>
> *(Pain, 2021, p. 976)*

It should be stated that acknowledging trauma as a normative feature of institutions is not an invitation to accept the problematic conclusion that "resistance to oppression is futile" (Oliver, 2004, p. 1). On the contrary, its commonness arguably warrants deeper resistance. The claim that trauma is an inherent product of institutional power enables such resistance by imagining trauma outside of the 'catastrophizing' logics of isolated events and ruptures that dog the psy disciplines (Stevens, 2011), and imagines responses otherwise. For instance, instead of focusing on resilience and recovery in the face of traumatic events (which are aimed at banishing trauma), this claim allows for an imagining of institutional resistance that stays with and addresses trauma. The conceptual tools I discuss here therefore imagine ways to resist trauma on an institutional basis. I will first discuss tools for resistance against – and imagination beyond – the dominance of individualized, psychiatrized, and pathologizing understandings of trauma that function to isolate and silence those who experience trauma. These come in the form of *melancholy* and *psychiatric abolition*. I will then discuss one final tool for resistance against experiences of trauma as they are institutionally enabled but not institutionally addressed. This final tool comes in the form of *justice by any means*.

Melancholy

The first conceptual tool that may be invoked in response to the third claim is *melancholy*. This is the first of two conceptual tools I will discuss for resistance against – and imagination beyond – dominant individualized, psychiatrized, and pathologizing understandings of trauma. In Robin James' consideration of resilience discourse, which I discussed in Chapters 3 and 5, James argues that resilience discourse operates in service to *Multi-Racial White Supremacist Patriarchy* (MRWaSP) by forcing bodies to endure and manage the violence of such conditions. In response, James (2015) argues for a need to resist MRWaSP by developing "critical and counter-hegemonic *alternatives* to and *maladaptations* of resilience" (p. 166):

> If resilience is a technique for investing in the *life* of MRWaSP, then perhaps making *bad investments*... ...would suck the life out of, rather than support, MRWaSP.
> *(James, 2015, p. 166)*

Here, *melancholy* is articulated as a "tactic of counter-resilience" (James, 2015, p. 19). This is in contrast with – and resistance against – traditional pathologizing formulations of *melancholia* in the psy disciplines, which refer to an inability to 'get over' or resolve loss (James, 2015) (which, uncoincidentally, is deployed in neoliberal recovery imperatives). Instead, James (2015) articulates melancholy as a refusal to invest in resilience and its (re)productions of established power, affirming that "melancholy is failed or inefficient self-capitalization" (James, 2015, p. 141). Here, melancholy is viewed not in opposition to resilience, but as a subversion of it; a refusal to invest in the imperative for self-capitalization and self-transformation that is the 'life force' of neoliberalism's biopolitics. In other words, melancholy is viewed as an antidote to the imperative for resilience, which sustains MRWaSP.

As James (2015) explains, melancholy provides a critical analytic that enables broader resistance against biopolitical regulation. This is done by exposing resilience as a form of biopolitical control and imagining alternative ways of responding to the damages of such conditions:

> This biopolitical lens clarifies the distinction between resilience discourse, which is a specific ideology and technique, and the alternative ways of coping and recovery that oppressed groups have always used to survive amid the damage of racism, sexism, and so on.
>
> *(James, 2015, p. 166)*

Thus, melancholy offers a means of resistance against the isolating and silencing consequences of resilience by subverting the drive and requirement for resilience itself:

> If biopolitics incites everyone to live at a precisely-managed level of resilience or precarity, going into the death incites and intensifies individual-level phenomena so they produce an unviable, unhealthy mix or balance. The "death" we're going into here is not necessarily or even primarily about individuals – it's about biopolitical death, the unviability of a *population* tuned to optimize MRWaSP. In fact, one of the main ways to go into the death, to practice melancholic subversion, is to take care of yourself in non-resilient ways – for example, getting a regular, full night's sleep rather than constantly pushing the edge of burnout and exhaustion. *"Into the death" isn't about killing ourselves, it's about upsetting the balance of factors that contribute to the production of multi-racial white supremacist patriarchy and neoliberal capitalism*, making them unviable projects, bad investments, dead ends.
>
> *(James, 2015, p. 20-1)*

When the 'life' of biopolitics under MRWaSP is embodied and sustained by resilience, then, melancholy invites us into the 'death of biopolitics' in two ways. First, melancholy invites us into the 'death' of biopolitics by refusing or subverting resilience. Here, embodying melancholy means rejecting dominant requirements of 'life' and embodying biopolitical definitions of 'death.' Second melancholy invites us into the 'death of biopolitics' by refusing to invest in these modes of regulation in ways that 'corrupt' and 'suck the life out' of them. As James puts it:

> "dying" means living a supposedly unviable life, a life that isn't profitable for MRWaSP, a life whose support diminishes the resilience of other, more elite groups. What happens when we invest in unviable, unprofitable lives? Can going *into the death* corrupt resilience discourse?
>
> *(James, 2015, p. 50)*

Here, James (2015) invites imaginations of resistance against and beyond the institutions that benefit and profit from resilience. Within such imaginations, melancholy constitutes a withdrawal of labor from the practices that sustain such institutions (e.g., MRWaSP). Thus, as a subversion of resilience, melancholy allows for institutional resistance against – and imagination beyond – dominant responses that locate individuals as the site of trauma and its management and sell resilience back to them as 'empowerment.' As such, melancholy operates as an alternative to resilience discourse, inviting us to stay with the damage of MRWaSP in ways that do not resolve it, but rather open up ways to resist these institutions and the logics that uphold them. Here, it is possible to imagine responses to trauma beyond their confines.

Psychiatric Abolition

The second conceptual tool that may be invoked in response to the third claim is *psychiatric abolition*. This is the second conceptual tool I will discuss for resistance against – and imagination beyond – dominant individualized, psychiatrized, and pathologizing understandings of trauma. It is a conceptual tool that specifically allows imagination beyond the *Trauma ⇔ PTSD* interpretative framework. Critical psychologists have identified and affirmed both the need for – and the challenges of – resistance against the impositions of the psy disciplines and their diagnostic frameworks. Indeed, as Ian Parker and colleagues have noted, "critiques of psychiatric discourse and clinical practice always have to contend with a range of excuses and defences from those who collude with, or even actively employ, traditional notions of psychopathology" (Parker et al. 1995, p. 119). I invoke *psychiatric abolition* in light of these observations and in expectation of resistance, recognizing that this only serves to further demonstrate its need.

(De)Theorizing and (Re)Imagining Institutional Trauma   129

As discussed throughout this book, dominant psychiatric perspectives have largely banished the kinds of considerations that would allow for the imagination of an institutional analytic of trauma. This can be seen in the individualized, medicalized, and symptoms-based interpretations of – and responses to – trauma discussed in Chapters 2 and 3. These dominant perspectives adopt a medical model in response to trauma, which constructs trauma primarily as a physical condition or disease through the dominant diagnostic category of PTSD. While the assumption that psychiatric conditions are "equivalent to physical diseases" has been heavily contested (Moncrieff, 2010, p. 370), this assumption nevertheless underpins an empire that has been built around diagnostic classificatory systems and their applications. Here, psychiatric diagnosis has been presented as a branch of medical diagnosis more broadly and is presumed to be grounded in medical facts, where diagnosis "covers both the process of identifying a disease, and the designation of that disease" (Moncrieff, 2010, p. 371). However – as discussed in Chapter 3 – because the DSM's classifications do not describe nor provide comprehensive evidence of biological pathologies (Bonanno, 2021), psychiatric practice has been criticized for "dressing up normative judgements about behaviour as medical facts" (Moncrieff, 2010, p. 371). In response, critical scholars have identified a substantial "gulf between what psychiatric diagnosis purports to be and how it functions in everyday practice" (Moncrieff, 2010, p. 371).

In response, calls have been made for alternatives to the medicalized psychiatric models used to interpret psychological distress. In her *counterhegemonic* response to psychiatry (Burstow, 2019, p. 1), Bonnie Burstow advocates for loosening the grip of psychiatry and offers an invitation to imagine what a paradigm shift might look like. In doing so, she invokes the negative space of psychiatric abolition, or ways to imagine psychic distress outside of and beyond dominant psychiatric frameworks and institutions. Burstow (2019) organizes this invitation around observations of the harms done by dominant medicalized paradigms, and invites resistance in response. In a similar vein, Emily O (2023) imagines psychiatric abolition as an expansion beyond institutions that are "*designed* to inflict violence, coercion and restraint" (Emily O, 2023, para 2). Along these lines, she argues that "abolition is not just about destruction, but about expansion. It gives us new ways, not only of thinking, but of doing too" (para 1).

It is important to note that the arguments made in this chapter are specifically concerned with notions of trauma, and not the full gamut of diagnostic categories. Each of these deserves their own attention. However, trauma is specifically apt to psychiatric abolition because it is both a heavily situated and relational phenomenon, and has been a specific domain of psychiatric pathologization and harm. Burstow (2005) argues on these grounds that the PTSD diagnosis is both "untenable and undesirable" (p. 431). Others have elucidated such harms in studies of trauma-related therapeutic practice, showing that medicalized responses within the PTSD framework serve to support the widespread administration of psychopharmaceuticals that carry a range of harmful impacts. For instance, ethnographic research from Spring (2016) with military veterans documents the extensive physiological and relational harms of drugs routinely prescribed for the treatment of PTSD. On these grounds, psychiatric abolition – in relation to trauma – is specifically concerned with expanding understandings of trauma *beyond* the biopsychiatric realms and harms of the PTSD category. In dialogue about the impacts of abuse, Burstow observes that this necessarily involves a loosening of the *Trauma* ⇔ *PTSD* interpretative framework:

> there is no problem whatever with you talking about this and using the word "trauma". On the other hand, there *is* a problem with you using the term "PTSD" or "Posttraumatic Stress Disorder". Insofar as you use such terms, you are calling people's natural responses to the terrible things that have happened to them a disorder.
> *(Burstow, 2019, p. 145)*

In response, it has been argued that trauma and posttraumatic stress could be imagined in a range of other ways. For example, Muldoon et al. (2021) argue that trauma can be understood as inextricable from a person's social identity and positioning within broader socio-political relations, which shape the availability of justice. With a specific focus on the social dimensions of posttraumatic stress, the authors argue that "power and politics become embedded in different trauma trajectories" (Muldoon et al. 2021, p. 510). On this basis, the authors argue that "to emphasize the role of individual pathologies, while neglecting the role played by wider societal practices and structural factors that contribute to the generation and management of trauma compromises both our scientific understanding and good practice" (Muldoon et al. 2021, p. 524). The authors therefore advocate for perspectives that look at trauma beyond medicalized frameworks and individual symptoms, with a specific focus on institutions.

Since the early 2000s, there have also been calls for practice-based responses beyond these frameworks. Burstow (2003) has called for "more radical counselling" (p. 1293) in response to trauma. Such practices, Burstow argues, should 'rupture' the hold of the DSM and

PTSD category on trauma and "break with psychiatry" (Burstow, 2003, p. 1301). Articulating this 'break,' she argues that:

> What is involved here is not expending energy tampering with the *DSM*, not using a deficiency model, not framing psychological and social problems in terms of diagnostic categories, and ridding practice of medical language such as *recovery*, *symptoms*, and *diagnoses* and all diagnostic names including PTSD.
> *(Burstow, 2003, p. 1301)*

This might involve approaching trauma as a continuum, "inviting clients to see themselves on a trauma continuum on which everyone is located" (Burstow, 2003, p. 1311), and addressing responses to trauma not as 'symptoms' to be eradicated, but as ways of coping that reflect certain requirements to cope and serve legitimate purposes. Others have argued that responses to trauma need to address legacies of patriarchy, capitalism, and coloniality (Segalo, 2015; Segalo & Fine, 2020). Indeed, without such recognition of histories and legacies of violence, "there can be no collective framework of intelligibility for survivors' privately lived experiences" (Segalo, 2015, p. 448). In their work on dialogicity in psychiatric practice, Seikkula and Arnkil (2006) provide an analytic that could be applied in ways that focus on the relational dimensions of trauma, arguing that "people live in social relations even if professionals are approaching them individually" (p. 1). Their approach replaces a focus on symptoms and pathology with a focus on dialogue. Here, dialogue is imagined as a forum in which new understandings and meanings of experiences can be generated between participants. Here, "the entire interaction system becomes our focus, not just specific therapeutic techniques" (p. 104). Such an approach could allow for new modes of meaning-making to become available outside of dominant individualized paradigms. Here, institutional frameworks, processes, and practices come into focus as sites of intervention and transformation.

Justice by Any Means

The third conceptual tool that may be invoked in response to the third claim is *justice by any means*. This tool is taken up from feminist psychological work by Aaronette White and Shagun Rastogi (2009), and is invoked in resistance against experiences of trauma as they are institutionally enabled but not institutionally addressed. Specifically, the notion of *justice by any means*, is invoked in response to observations throughout this book that legal and criminal justice institutions function to tightly regulate understandings and experiences of trauma, constrain how trauma can be addressed, and harm those who are seeking justice. For instance, as discussed in Chapter 3, criminal justice processes are routinely weaponized and wielded against those they purport to serve (Reeves et al. 2023). Also discussed in Chapter 3, law can have a silencing effect, locking stories of trauma away behind closed doors. This is a problem because criminal justice, coordinated by the institution of law, is the dominant pathway for seeking *justice* in response to trauma. Therefore, culturally approved modes of justice – obtainable strictly through the institution of law – are insufficient and problematic. This creates and sustains a set of dominant conditions in which trauma is institutionally enabled but not institutionally addressed. In response, feminist psychologists have advocated for expansions of justice in recognition of the need for justice in the absence of justice (White & Rastogi, 2009). Based on an absence or corruption of formal pathways to justice, White and Rastogi (2009) advocate for *justice by any means necessary*. In doing so, they consider different modes of grassroots justice, including restorative justice, retributive justice, and vigilantism. White and Rastogi (2009) define retribution in this context as "a wish to vindicate the value of the victim and the community as a whole" (p. 316), and a way to "integrate broad structural injustices and local everyday injustices in... efforts at social change" (p. 317). In this work, the authors examined acts of grassroots retribution and vigilantism among women in India who were "already excluded from the barely functioning aspects of the judicial systems in their localities" (p. 318). This included collective confrontations in response to violent husbands, men who demanded sexual favors in exchange for access to basic resources, and land-grabbing 'thugs' (White & Rastogi, 2009). In doing so, the authors articulate how – in an absence of formal justice – expanded forms of grassroots retribution and vigilantism can arise in response to institutionally enabled harm that is not institutionally addressed:

> Women presented here live under violent circumstances whether they fight back or not; multiple patriarchies inadvertently and repeatedly condone men's violence against women. As a result, some women disrupt this power dynamic by relearning their propensity for violence. Although women reclaiming the ability and right to use force will not by itself end patriarchy, it may be a useful form of empowerment and protection in the short term when accompanied by a long-term liberatory vision.
>
> *(White & Rastogi, 2009, p. 318)*

Here, grassroots retribution and vigilantism serve as collective, community responses to institutionally enabled harm, recognizing both the absence of institutional support and the institutional origins of harm. Due to the absences, inadequacies, and harms of criminal justice responses, grassroots retribution opens up potentials to respond to violence directly as an institutional phenomenon and *by any means* necessary. Here, the institution becomes the site of intervention, be it through the transformation of institutionalized modes of justice into grassroots practices, or the deep recognition that everyday injustices are structural injustices. And, while the authors recognize that this form of grassroots justice "will not by itself end patriarchy" (White & Rastogi, 2009, p. 318), they do recognize that a range of grassroots practices enable everyday resistance against the violences of patriarchy. The expansion of justice *by any means* is therefore a valuable analytic, which can be applied in instances of institutionally enabled trauma that is not institutionally addressed. The goal here is to imagine justice beyond the confines of prevailing institutions and find justice by other means.

Conclusion

This chapter has considered some ways of approaching trauma beyond medicalized frameworks and individual symptoms, with a specific focus on institutions. Moving beyond these boundaries, this institutional analytic of trauma has brought a range of possibilities into view for understanding trauma as an institutional phenomenon, moving beyond dominant assumptions about how to understand and respond to trauma. This has been an investigation of the *negative space* surrounding trauma. Here, I have invoked a range of conceptual tools that allow for institutional exploration, intervention, and transformation. These tools do not lay claim to trauma in universalizing ways, nor are they comprehensive. Rather, they enable ways into the negative space surrounding dominant conceptualizations of trauma. Chapter 7 will now serve as a portal into this negative space by considering the potentials for imagination and justice that reside there.

References

Ahmed, S. (2012). *On Being Included: Racism and Diversity in Institutional Life*. Duke University Press.

Ahmed, S. (2017). *Living a Feminist Life*. Duke University Press.

Alcoff, L. M. (2007). Epistemologies of Ignorance: Three Types. In S. Sullivan & N. Tuana (Eds.), *Race and Epistemologies of Ignorance* (pp. 39–58). State University of New York Press.

Ali, S. S., Lifshitz, M., & Raz, A. (2014). Empirical neuroenchantment: From reading minds to thinking critically. *Frontiers in Human Neuroscience*, 8(MAY). https://doi.org/10.3389/fnhum.2014.00357

Bhatia, S., Long, W., Pickren, W., & Rutherford, A. (2024). Engaging with decoloniality, decolonization, and histories of psychology otherwise. In L. Comas-Díaz, H. Y. Adames, & N. Y. Chavez-Dueñas (Eds.), *Decolonial psychology: Toward anticolonial theories, research, training, and practice* (pp. 61–85). American Psychological Association. https://doi.org/10.1037/0000376-004

Bonanno, G. A. (2021). *The End of Trauma: How the New Science of Resilience is Changing how we Think About PTSD*. Basic Books.

Burstow, B. (2003). Toward a radical understanding of trauma and trauma work. *Violence against Women*, 9(11), 1293–1317. https://doi.org/10.1177/1077801203255555

Burstow, B. (2005). A critique of posttraumatic stress disorder and the DSM. *Journal of Humanistic Psychology*, 45(4), 429–445. https://doi.org/10.1177/0022167805280265

Burstow, B. (2019). *The Revolt Against Psychiatry: A Counterhegemonic Dialogue*. Palgrave Macmillan.

Ehrkamp, P., Loyd, J. M., & Secor, A. J. (2022). Trauma as displacement: Observations from refugee resettlement. *Annals of the American Association of Geographers*, 112(3), 715–722.

Emily O. (2023). Another way is possible. *Asylum: A Radical Mental Health Magazine*, 14–15.

Fine, M., & McClelland, S. I. (2006). Sexuality education and desire: Still missing after all these Yyears. *Harvard Educational Review*, 76(3), 297–338.

Gallagher, S. (2013). A pattern theory of self. *Frontiers in Human Neuroscience*, 7, 1–7. https://doi.org/10.3389/fnhum.2013.00443

Gallagher, S., & Daly, A. (2018). Dynamical relations in the self-pattern. *Frontiers in Psychology*, 9(MAY). https://doi.org/10.3389/fpsyg.2018.00664

Geertz, C. (1973). Thick Description: Toward an Interpretive Theory of Culture. In C. Geertz (Ed.), *The Interpretation of Cultures* (pp. 3–30). Basic Books.

Henriques, J., Hollway, W., Urwin, C., Venn, C., & Walkerdine, V. (1984). Introduction: The Point of Departure. In J. Henriques, W. Hollway, C. Urwin, C. Venn, & V. Walkerdine (Eds.), *Changing the Subject: Psychology, Social Regulation and Subjectivity* (pp. 1–9). Methuen & Co. Ltd.

James, R. (2015). *Resilience & Melancholy: Pop Music, Feminism, Neoliberalism*. Zero Books.

Kriss, S. (2013, October 18). Book of Lamentations. The New Inquiry. https://thenewinquiry.com/book-of-lamentations/

Liebert, R. J. (2019). *Psycurity*. Routledge.

Moncrieff, J. (2010). Psychiatric diagnosis as a political device. *Social Theory and Health*, 8(4), 370–382. https://doi.org/10.1057/sth.2009.11

Muldoon, O. T., Lowe, R. D., Jetten, J., Cruwys, T., & Haslam, S. A. (2021). Personal and political: Post-traumatic stress through the lens of social identity, power, and politics. *Political Psychology*, 42(3), 501–533. https://doi.org/10.1111/pops.12709

Oliver, K. (2004). *The Colonization of Psychic Space: A Psychoanalytic Social Theory of Oppression*. University of Minnesota Press.
Pain, R. (2021). Geotrauma: Violence, place and repossession. *Progress in Human Geography*, 45(5), 972–989. https://doi.org/10.1177/0309132520943676
Parker, I., Georgaca, E., Harper, D., McLaughlin, T., & Stowell-Smith, M. (1995). *Deconstructing Psychopathology*. Sage Publications.
Reeves, E., Fitz-Gibbon, K., Meyer, S., & Walklate, S. (2023). Incredible women: Legal systems abuse, coercive control, and the credibility of victim-survivors. *Violence Against Women*, 31(3–4), 767–788. https://doi.org/10.1177/10778012231220370
Sedgwick, E. K. (2003). *Touching Feeling: Affect, Pedagogy, Performativity*. Duke University Press.
Segalo, P. (2015). Trauma and gender. *Social and Personality Psychology Compass*, 9(9), 447–454. https://doi.org/10.1111/spc3.12192
Segalo, P., & Fine, M. (2020, May 29). *Critical inquiry on gendered violence in the global north and south: A conversation between Puleng Segalo and Michelle Fine [Keynote Presentation]*. The Psychology of Global Crises, Paris, France. https://www.youtube.com/watch?reload=9&v=lR6jVG7W6rE
Seikkula, J., & Arnkil, T. E. (2006). *Dialogical Meetings in Social Networks*. H. Karnac (Books) Ltd.
Smith, D. E. (1987). *The Everyday World as Problematic: A Feminist Sociology*. Northeastern University Press.
Smith, D. E. (2005). *Institutional Ethnography: A Sociology for People*. Rowman & Littlefield Publishers, Inc.
Smith, D. E. (2006). Introduction. In D. E. Smith (Ed.), *Institutional Ethnography as Practice* (pp. 1–11). Rowman & Littlefield Publishers, Inc.
Smith, D. E., & Griffith, A. I. (2022). *Simply Institutional Ethnography*. University of Toronto Press.
Spring, L. (2016). Pathologizing Military Trauma: How Services Members, Veterans, and Those Who Care About Them Fall Prey to Institutional Capture and the DSM. In B. Burstow (Ed.), *Psychiatry Interrogated: An Institutional Ethnography Anthology* (pp. 125–142). Palgrave Macmillan.
Stevens, M. E. (2011). Trauma's Essential Bodies. In M. J. Casper & P. Currah (Eds.), *Corpus: An Interdisciplinary Reader on Bodies and Knowledge* (pp. 171–186). Palgrave Macmillan.
Stevens, M. E. (2016). Trauma Is as Trauma Does: The Politics of Affect in Catastrophic Times. In M. J. Casper & E. Wertheimer (Eds.), *Critical Trauma Studies: Understanding Violence, Memory, and Conflict in Everyday Life* (pp. 19–36). New York University Press.
Thompson, L. (2021). Toward a feminist psychological theory of "institutional trauma." *Feminism & Psychology*, 31(1), 99–118. https://doi.org/10.1177/0959353520968374
Wertheimer, E., & Casper, M. J. (2016). Within Trauma: An Introduction. In E. Wertheimer & M. J. Casper (Eds.), *Critical Trauma Studies: Understanding Violence, Conflict, and Memory in Everyday Life* (pp. 1–16). New York University Press.
White, A., & Rastogi, S. (2009). Justice by any means necessary: Vigilantism among Indian women. *Feminism and Psychology*, 19(3), 313–327. https://doi.org/10.1177/0959353509105622

Wynter, S. (2003). Unsettling the coloniality of being/power/truth/freedom: Towards the human, after man, its overrepresentation—an argument. *CR: The New Centennial Review*, 3(3), 257–337.

Younas, A., Fàbregues, S., Durante, A., Escalante, E. L., Inayat, S., & Ali, P. (2023). Proposing the "MIRACLE" narrative framework for providing thick description in qualitative research. *International Journal of Qualitative Methods*, 22. https://doi.org/10.1177/16094069221147162

7
INTO TRAUMA'S NEGATIVE SPACE

I am a critical feminist psychologist who studies institutional dynamics, and somebody who has been through psychiatric diagnostic systems and therapeutic responses to trauma. I have dealt with a great deal of distress from the fundamental lack of recognition that the *personal is political* in therapeutic spaces, psychological theory, and popular discourse. I don't think I am alone in this distress. I also don't think you need to be a critical feminist psychologist to feel this way. My experiences of distress and fear are so heavily lodged in the knowledge that institutional conditions enabled what happened, and that these conditions remain in place and intact. I don't think I am alone in this knowledge, and it is jarring to me that this is not well-recognized in institutional responses. And, while some individualized modes of therapeutic support have been helpful, I have struggled to find support that recognizes and addresses the personal-political dynamics of my distress. I have also struggled to find any support that does not ultimately interpret my distress through dominant biopsychiatric frameworks. This has amounted to an overwhelming experience of distress in response to the process of pathologization, which feels profoundly wrong. This book is, in part, a reflexive response to this distress.

It is also a mode of hopeful speculation about how trauma might be imagined otherwise. It is an invitation into the *negative space* surrounding dominant conceptualizations of trauma: the space that falls out of view while also operating to give shape and meaning to dominant frameworks. Here, I imagine this negative space as institutional. Venturing into this negative space allows for a focus on the institutional forces that give dominant interpretations of trauma their shape and meaning, and imaginations of trauma as an institutional phenomenon. On this basis, this book has been an exercise in seeing what comes into view with an institutional focus. This has been done through an unraveling of dominant trauma knowledges based on the observation that they are

DOI: 10.4324/9781003042471-7

institutionally produced, and an invitation to imagine understandings and experiences of trauma as institutionally bound.

This book therefore constitutes a different orientation to trauma, focused not on individuals and their symptoms but on institutions and their role in the (re)production of trauma. In this chapter, I will consider what it means to explore the *negative space* of trauma and imagine trauma otherwise. As such, this chapter serves not as a review or conclusion, but as a portal into the possibilities of this negative space. Here, I advocate against theoretical formalization, instead inviting ongoing and collective explorations of the possibilities for institutional understanding and transformation that come into view through such explorations. The unraveling and imagining undertaken here to loosen dominant interpretations therefore brings us to 'loose ends.' Therefore, rather than simply serving as the 'end' of this book, this chapter is a launching point into the negative space of institutions.

Into Trauma's Negative Space

In the *positive space* of trauma, individualized interpretations are sharply in focus and the individual has been rendered in great detail as both the site of trauma and the obvious target of intervention and transformation on this basis. In this book, I have reasserted the observation that *the personal is political*. As I have argued previously, trauma is a deeply personal experience, but it is not located in a vacuum (Thompson, 2021). By imagining trauma in a vacuum, dominant approaches have foreclosed possibilities to imagine this space otherwise. If this supposed 'vacuum' does not exist – and instead there are a set of complex institutional conditions that give trauma its shape and meaning – we are presented with a realm of imagination that was previously cut off.

Imagination

Such foreclosures can be viewed as a consequence of the epistemic dominance of Euro-American science in the psy disciplines, which have overseen the erasure of a range of knowledges (Gone, 2021; Liebert, 2019). Beyond the privileging of particular ideas and frameworks over others, critical psychologists have argued that this epistemic dominance has also been reproduced through practices of 'Knowing' (Liebert, 2019) that have subjugated other modes of thought, which "blocks, refuses, ignores other worlds" (Liebert, 2019, p. 110). Dominant interpretative frameworks of trauma (as discussed in Chapter 2) are particularly problematic in this sense because they locate trauma within individuals while at the same time casting inflicted individuals as unable to know their trauma. This creates and bolsters the position of 'experts' within prevailing hierarchies of knowledge and knowing. More than this, it also coerces us into 'Knowing' only on these terms, operating as "a sort of (En)light(ened) pollution that stops us from seeing the stars" (Liebert, 2019, p. 110). As such, it has been argued that epistemic dominance has accomplished a form of psychic colonization through the destruction of imagination itself:

> critical psychologists from around the world name the destruction of imagination as central to the colonization of the psyche, such that imagining itself has become a present-day decolonizing praxis.
> *(Liebert, 2019, p. 110)*

Imagination beyond these confines, then, offers possibilities to see things otherwise. This book has been an exercise in this kind of imagination, arguing against a singular mode of 'Knowing' (Liebert, 2019) that forecloses and invites hostility toward other interpretations (Fassin & Rechtman, 2009). In this sense, the practice of imagining in trauma's negative space allows resistance against the forms of psychologization, pathologization, and privatization that foreclose institutional imaginings. Brought into circulation by the Euro-American colonial sciences, these forms of psychic regulation constitute not only a narrowing of focus to individuals and their pathologies, but also an imposition of standards of 'Knowing' that devalue and eradicate others. More broadly, these modes of regulation have also delimited possibilities for action. In line with these assumptions, millions of people are encouraged every day to go to private therapy, for instance. The specific form of privatization accomplished through these foreclosures of imagination has stifled collective and institutional responses.

Imagination has been considered a central tool for resistance against such foreclosures and the erasures they accomplish. Against privatization, Glăveanu et al. (2025) discuss 'imagination practice,' based on the notion of *ecologies of collective imagination*. Here, the authors argue that collective imagination is a hopeful practice that engages those who have been marginalized as 'knowers' in processes of justice:

> collective forms of imagination can engage individuals in actions related to environmental awareness and reparative justice, including ways of widening participation by engaging people who may have been excluded from the power of ecological learning and imagination, ultimately building aspiration and responding to change to

build hope for the future. The premise of this project is that human lives are lived in the realm of the possible as much as they are in the here-and-now of immediate experience of the more-than-human world.

(Glăveanu et al., 2025, p. 1)

Here, we can imagine the negative space of trauma as the "realm of the possible" in contrast with prevailing interpretations, which might constitute the "here-and-now of immediate experience" (Glăveanu et al., 2025, p. 1). Against privatization, the authors argue that the practice of collective imagination can open up space for the generation of new possibilities for understanding and relating to the world. Imagination in this way engages people who may have been excluded from the possibilities of imagining. Specifically, in the case of trauma, this offers possibilities to rupture the epistemic dominance that shuts down imagination. In doing so, imagination practices could bring those who are denied the capacity to 'Know' into dialogue about these possibilities, offering ways to pursue modes of understanding and justice that otherwise remain foreclosed.

Hermeneutical Justice

As I argued in Chapter 1, Miranda Fricker has observed that epistemic dominance controls the forms of understanding and interpretation that are made available in broader cultural spaces, where "the powerful have an unfair advantage in structuring collective social understandings" (Fricker, 2007, p. 148). This creates a set of conditions wherein "flaws in shared interpretive resources prevent the subject from making sense of an experience," rendering this unintelligible (Fricker, 2007, p. 148). As Stevens (2016) observes, this extends to understandings of the self and our positionality in the world:

> narratives of individual and community "self-hood" provide us with ideas about who we are, or think we are, and present us with visions of our place in the cosmos, in history, in society, and in doing so relate us to our own sense of interiority. These are narratives of the past, the present, and the future, and they are routed through myriad forms of material, ultimately coming to constitute our sense of identity. These are narratives of science, religion, history, memory, politics, and psyche, and, in their own way, they provide the content that is drawn up, absorbed into, and constitutive of social relations, knowledge objects, and institutions, the operations of which we study and engage.
>
> *(Stevens, 2016, p. 19)*

Hermeneutical injustice arises when those dominant forms of interpretation render others unavailable, constraining how a particular experience, phenomenon, or mode of selfhood can be understood (Fricker, 2007). Being denied the capacity to 'Know' can also be viewed as a form of hermeneutical injustice in and of itself. As hermeneutics refers to interpretation, hermeneutical injustice refers to a politics of interpretation whereby dominant interpretations shut down others that may be beneficial. As Fricker (2007) argues:

> relations of unequal power can skew shared hermeneutical resources so that the powerful tend to have appropriate understandings of their experiences ready to draw on as they make sense of their social experiences, whereas the powerless are more likely to find themselves having some social experiences through a glass darkly, with at best ill-fitting meanings to draw on in the effort to render them intelligible.
> *(Fricker, 2007, p. 148)*

This is certainly true of the best-selling books on trauma and the epistemologies of ignorance on which they stand; written from the most privileged perspectives and fundamentally dedicated to the (re)production of evermore detailed and de-politicized renderings of individuals. How – in the face of brutal institutional and state violence – can trauma simply be approached as a medical concern? This question is both rhetorical and haunting.

In Chapter 1, I considered how dominant psychological frameworks have given rise to hermeneutical injustice, with Khúc (2024) observing that:

> the stories I had been told… were not only wrong but also the very structures that shaped why life felt unlivable for me. And so I turned my eye to those stories and asked where they came from, and how they harm…
>
> I asked, what else is hurting us, invisibly, that we internalize as individual pathology to be individually overcome? I asked, what alternative stories might we tell about ourselves, about our suffering and our healing, and what new languages would we need to do so?
> *(Khúc, 2024, p. 9)*

Here, Khúc (2024) invites us into the negative space outside of dominant pathologizing interpretations of psychological distress, asking "what alternative stories might we tell about ourselves…" and "what new languages would we need to do so?" (Khúc, 2024, p. 9). Such counternarratives and languages are offered as ways into imagining distress outside of everyday interpretations that are both 'wrong,' and part of the architectures of dominance that make life 'unlivable' (Khúc, 2024, p. 9). Here, negative space offers a way out of these 'wrong' and 'unlivable' frameworks by turning away from them and rendering others intelligible. In the negative space of trauma, this invites questions over the alternative stories and languages that might render other modes of interpretation and understanding visible. In Chapter 6, I discussed several conceptual tools that might be invoked to these ends.

There is also hermeneutical injustice in silence. Indeed, silence halts alternative stories and new languages, ensuring the preservation of prevailing interpretations. In Chapter 3, I argued for this reason that justice resides in the battle against silence. In relation to public survivor-led movements like Time's Up™ and #MeToo, I discussed the observation that "this surge in public sharing of trauma stories is a rhetorical form of resistance to ideologies in mainstream American culture that impose silence on survivors" (Delker et al., 2020, p. 242). As rhetorical resistance, these movements can be understood as a form of hermeneutical resistance against modes of understanding that impose silence. The recognition of hermeneutical injustice here lies in the observation that certain ideologies impose silence. Hermeneutical justice offers possibilities to intervene in institutional dominance and the "colonization of the psyche" (Liebert, 2019, p. 110) that is accomplished therein. As one form of *justice by any means*, then, hermeneutical justice can be understood as a mode of *justice by imagination* outside of such dominance, and therefore in the *negative space* of trauma.

Loose ends

As this book has shown, entering the *negative space* of trauma involves unraveling epistemic dominance and imagining trauma otherwise to loosen dominant theory and focus attention beyond these realms. This is especially necessary in light of the absences of justice and "epistemologies of ignorance" (Alcoff, 2007, p. 39) that deflect attention away from such matters. While I have discussed some conceptual tools that may allow for explorations of this negative space, these are not comprehensive – nor should they be. Unraveling epistemic dominance gives us threads to follow, not tie up with certainty. As such, the negative space of trauma brings us to 'loose ends,' or strands of exploration that are open – not closed – to interpretation. As such, this loosening becomes a means to loose ends.

In this book, I have intentionally avoided giving a singular definition of trauma precisely for this reason. Rather, I have articulated how trauma slides between formal definition, contestation, and refutation, which makes it impossible to 'Know' in one way. This is in direct contradiction with dominant modes of 'Knowing' (Liebert, 2019), which operate on a distinct mode of certainty. Specifically, I have drawn on *critical trauma studies* (Stevens, 2016) to develop such a view, observing the central argument that:

> *trauma* is not simply a concept that describes particularly overwhelming events, nor is it simply a category that "holds" people who have been undone by such events; but it is a cultural object whose function produces particular types of subjects, and predisposes specific affect flows that it then manages and ultimately shunts into political projects of various types.
>
> *(Stevens, 2016, p. 20)*

In response, I stay with *not knowing* as a form of resistance against dominant modes of certainty that claim to 'Know' the phenomenon of trauma. Recognizing that "trauma is as trauma does" (Stevens, 2016, p. 19), loose ends bring possibilities to understand trauma as it is imagined and experienced in a range of ways. As such, these loose ends proliferate in negative space. In this book, *negative space* has been understood as a realm where institutions come into view as sites of trauma and its management, beyond theoretical constraint and dominance. Decoupling understandings of trauma from the individualizing logics of diagnostic practice and biological (mal)adaptation, this negative space and its loose ends turn our attention to understanding trauma as it is produced, situated, felt, and negotiated through the very institutions that would have us believe it is our problem – and ours alone – to fix. This vast unraveling therefore serves as a starting point for serious explorations of trauma, violence, harm, and justice in the many realms of negative space that have hitherto been closed off.

References

Alcoff, L. M. (2007). Epistemologies of Ignorance: Three Types. In S. Sullivan & N. Tuana (Eds.), *Race and Epistemologies of Ignorance* (pp. 39–58). State University of New York Press.

Delker, B. C., Salton, R., & McLean, K. C. (2020). Giving voice to silence: Empowerment and disempowerment in the developmental shift from trauma 'victim' to 'survivor-advocate'. *Journal of Trauma and Dissociation, 21*(2), 242–263. https://doi.org/10.1080/15299732.2019.1678212

Fassin, D., & Rechtman, R. (2009). *The Empire of Trauma*. Princeton University Press.

Fricker, M. (2007). *Epistemic Injustice: Power and the Ethics of Knowing*. Oxford University Press.

Glăveanu, V., Hay, P., McDowall, H., Doust, T., Welles, S., Chaudhuri, G., Pender, A., & Hurley, M. (2025). Ecologies of collective imagination. *International Journal of Art and Design Education*. https://doi.org/10.1111/jade.12568

Gone, J. P. (2021). Decolonization as methodological innovation in counseling psychology: Method, power, and process in reclaiming american indian therapeutic traditions. *Journal of Counseling Psychology*, 68(3), 259–270. https://doi.org/10.1037/cou0000500

Khúc, M. (2024). *Dear Elia: Letters from the Asian American Abyss*. Duke University Press.

Liebert, R. J. (2019). *Psycurity*. Routledge.

Stevens, M. E. (2016). Trauma Is as Trauma Does: The Politics of Affect in Catastrophic Times. In M. J. Casper & E. Wertheimer (Eds.), *Critical Trauma Studies: Understanding Violence, Memory, and Conflict in Everyday Life* (pp. 19–36). New York University Press.

Thompson, L. (2021). Toward a feminist psychological theory of "institutional trauma." *Feminism & Psychology*, 31(1), 99–118. https://doi.org/10.1177/0959353520968374

INDEX

ableism 53
Ahmed, S. 4–5; citation as feminist practice 10, 42; heterogender 75–78; institutions 68, 70, 84, 92, 122; 'overing' 62; personal as structural 4–5, 82; resilience 54–55; silence as violence 57–59; universal as specific 23
attachment theory 80–81

biopsychiatry 2–5, 19–21, 32, 34–35, 104, 137
body, the 24–28, 40, 106, 113
Bronfenbrenner, U. 97–98
Burman, E. 6–7, 29, 78–80, 82
Burstow, B. 52, 129–131

Carson, K. 16, 20, 54, 76–77
community psychology 97, 102
compulsory heterosexuality 76
critical trauma studies 106, 114, 124, 143
Curtis, A. 99–100
cybernetics 96–97

de-theorizing trauma 112–115
diagnostic imperialism 11, 39, 46, 95, 124; expansion of 46–47, 51, 71; self-diagnosis as 47
Diagnostic Statistical Manual of Mental Disorders (DSM) 41–44, 46, 51–52, 76, 114, 128–131
discourse 5–6, 69, 79–82; of colonialism 72; mainstream psychological 15–18; psychiatric 2–3

emplacements of trauma 123–125
epistemic injustice 9, 74–75, 140–142
Euro-American colonization 20, 71–73; scientific theory as 8–9, 73–75, 77, 112–113, 139
European enlightenment 16

family, the 78–81
Fanon, F. 72, 78, 82, 84
feminist psychological perspectives: on the family 78–79; principles of 5–7, 32, 68–70; on trauma 7–9, 29–32, 82–83; on violence 82–83, 131–133
Feminist Relational Discourse Analysis 5
Fricker, M. 9, 140

geotrauma 124
'get over it' discourse 61–62, 106, 126

Haaken, J. 20, 22, 23, 25–26, 28, 52
Herman, J. 80, 94
heterogender 75–80

imagination 138–140; justice by 142
individual psychological subject, the 17–18, 48–50, 54, 71–74, 94–95, 120–121
institutional betrayal theory 89–93
institutional ethnographies 121–123
institutional psychiatry 19

institutional trauma, definitions of 11–12, 15, 29, 32–35, 88, 103–106
intersectionality 34, 76

James, R. 54–55, 61, 126–128
justice by any means 131–133, 142

Leys, R. 1, 18, 23, 25–26
Liebert, R. J. 8–9; colonial hierarchies of 'Knowing' 29, 73–74, 107, 138–139, 143; imagination 72, 138–139; theory as colonization 110–113, 117, 120, 122, 142
loose ends 13, 138, 142–143

medicolegal discourse 25, 34, 58
melancholy 126–128
memory 21–22, 26–27, 90
mental health 2; campaigns 57; industry 45, 48; practices 6, 29, 44, 92–93, 124

negative space 10, 114–115; foreclosure of 107; as institutional 13, 63, 111–112, 137, 143; portals into 133, 138, 141–142; as resistance 129, 139–142
neocolonialism: trauma concept as 2, 10, 12, 35, 74, 110–111; global mental health as 45; as institution 68, 72–75, 93, 114; and violence 106
neoliberalism 48–50, 71–72, 103
neurobiology of trauma 24–28
neuroenchantment 28, 30, 116
'normality' *vs.* 'abnormality' 16–18, 41, 77, 115–116

office-based psychiatry 19

pain for sale 51
pathologization of trauma 2, 11, 21–23, 41–46, 137
pattern theory of self 120–121
personal is political, the 4–5, 7, 59, 70, 82, 137–138
postfeminism 55
posttraumatic growth 53–54
privatization of trauma 44–47, 56, 140
psychiatric abolition 128–131
psychiatrization of trauma 39–41, 71

psychopharmaceuticals 19, 24, 41–42, 51, 71, 130
psychotherapeutic intervention 40–41, 44, 48, 60
psy complex 41, 70–73, 84
PTSD (Post-Traumatic Stress Disorder) 21–24, 31, 34, 78, 95, 128–131

recovery imperative 60–62, 79, 126–128
resilience 41, 48, 53–63, 100–101, 126–128
Rose, N. 16; on diagnostic imperialism 39, 46; on the history of the psy disciplines 16–18, 71; on neoliberalism 48–50, 103; on the psychological subject 17–18, 120; on psychopathologization 21, 23, 41, 45

scientific classism 20–21, 34–35
scientific racism 20–21, 34–35
Segalo, P. 2–3; on neocolonialism 10, 12, 35, 74, 110–111, 131; on trauma 77–78, 119, 122
shell shock 22, 30
silence, cultures of 56–60, 62
speaking out 57–60
Stevens, M. E. 115, 140; body-as-text 24–27, 60; catastrophizing logics of trauma 25, 32, 40, 47–48, 71–72, 126; critique of PTSD 23–24; memory 26–27; the racialized Other 20–21, 34–35; trauma as cultural object 2, 30, 33–36, 48, 91, 143; trauma as institutional 104–106
stigmatization 4, 42–43
systemic trauma theory 89, 94–103
systems theory 96–98; critique of 98–103

thick description of trauma 117–119
Tosh, J. 8, 16, 20, 27, 54, 76–77
trauma capitalism 12, 39, 51, 72, 81; and cultures of silence 56–60; and recovery culture 60, 72; and resilience culture 53–55; tactics of 51–52
trauma industry 12, 39, 47–54
trauma-resilience-recovery pipeline 53, 60
trauma talk 30–31

TraumaTok 51
Tseris, E.: critique of biomedical approaches to trauma 3, 28–30, 43, 45–47, 51; definitions of trauma 1, 96; social complexities of trauma 11, 41, 47

universalism: in accounts of the body 24–27; and Euro-American dominance 10, 16, 73–74, 112; in psychological theory 6, 8, 10, 81, 117; rejection of 6, 8–10, 29, 120–121, 133; in trauma theory 8–11, 22–23, 28; in truth claims 5–6, 9; the universal as specific 6, 16, 23–25, 81, 119, 123

violence 4; colonial 77, 113; domestic 44, 106; epistemic 9; gender-based 5, 76–77, 132; honor-based 79; institutional 47, 55, 82–83, 126, 133; intimate partner 43, 79; police 5; sexual 32, 42, 79, 82–83, 106, 132; state 106, 132–133

weak theory 114–115
white ignorance 74
white supremacy 34, 68, 74, 112–113

For Product Safety Concerns and Information please contact our EU representative GPSR@taylorandfrancis.com Taylor & Francis Verlag GmbH, Kaufingerstraße 24, 80331 München, Germany

Printed and bound by CPI Group (UK) Ltd, Croydon, CR0 4YY

12/03/2026

02070562-0007